SCHOLASTIC CANADA

Children's
Atlas

of the
World

Scholastic Canada Ltd.
604 King Street West, Toronto, Ontario M5V 1E1, Canada

Scholastic Inc.
557 Broadway, New York, NY 10012, USA

Scholastic Australia Pty Limited
PO Box 579, Gosford, NSW 2250, Australia

Scholastic New Zealand Limited
Private Bag 94407, Greenmount, Auckland, New Zealand

Scholastic Children's Books
Euston House, 24 Eversholt Street, London NW1 1DB, UK

Cartography:
Digital Cartography supplied by Encompass Graphics Ltd, Hove, U.K.
Cartographic Consultant: Roger Bullen
Editorial Direction: Christiane Gunzi
Senior Editor: Louise Pritchard
Editorial Assistant: Katy Rayner
Art Direction: Chez Picthall
Design: Gillian Shaw and Paul Calver
Picture Research: Gillian Shaw and Katy Rayner
Map Indexing: Roger Bullen and Paula Metcalf
General Indexer: Angie Hipkin
Production: Toby Reynolds
Written by: Chez Picthall & Christiane Gunzi
Reproduction by Colourscan, Singapore

Created and produced by Picthall & Gunzi Limited
This edition published 2009 by Scholastic Canada Ltd.

Library and Archives Canada Cataloguing in Publication

Picthall, Chez
Scholastic Canada children's atlas of the world / Chez Picthall,
Christiane Gunzi.
ISBN 978-0-545-99307-4
1. Children's atlases. I. Gunzi, Christiane II. Title.
G1021.P45 2009   j912   C2008-907362-2

ISBN-10 0-545-99307-5

7 6 5 4 3 2   Printed in Malaysia   10 11 12 13 14

SCHOLASTIC CANADA

Children's
Atlas
of the
World

Chez Picthall

SCHOLASTIC CANADA LTD.

New York Toronto London Auckland Sydney
Mexico City New Delhi Hong Kong Buenos Aires

Contents

North America

South America

Africa

Europe

Asia

Oceania and the Pacific Islands

The Arctic and Antarctica

All about maps

Maps show us what places on Earth look like from above. They give useful information, such as where towns and cities are, or where rivers and mountains run. A map can help us to find out where we are and can show us the distances between places. Maps have to carry a lot of information, so different symbols, lines and colours are used to show the features on the Earth's surface. Symbols are often used to show the position of towns, and lines show where all the country borders and rivers are.

A street map

A country map

Map scales Maps are large- or small-scale. Large-scale maps show small areas with lots of detail, like the street map above. Small-scale maps show large areas with less detail, like this country map. All the maps in this atlas are small-scale.

How maps are made

The most accurate world maps are globes because they are the same shape as planet Earth. To make a flat map out of a globe, map-makers have to change the shape of Earth's surface. The land shapes get stretched and distorted. Map-makers do this work mathematically, using what is called a "projection." There are many different kinds of projection, and each one looks slightly different. The people who create maps are called "cartographers."

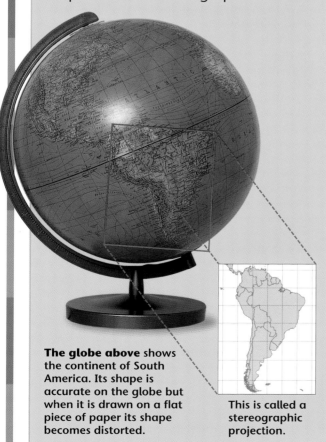

The globe above shows the continent of South America. Its shape is accurate on the globe but when it is drawn on a flat piece of paper its shape becomes distorted.

This is called a stereographic projection.

Latitude and longitude lines

To help us to locate places, we have invented invisible lines that run around the Earth. These are called the lines of latitude and longitude. Lines of latitude run horizontally. They measure how far north or south a place is from the Equator (around the Earth's middle). Longitude lines run from the North to the South Pole and measure how far east or west a place is from Greenwich, London. All these measurements are given in degrees and show a place's position on Earth.

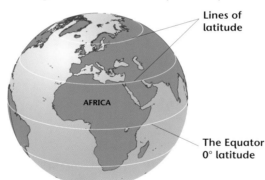

Lines of latitude

AFRICA

The Equator 0° latitude

Greenwich, London, UK 0° longitude

AFRICA

Lines of longitude

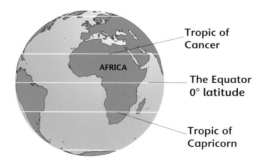

Tropic of Cancer

AFRICA

The Equator 0° latitude

Tropic of Capricorn

The Equator and the Tropics

The Equator is an imaginary line that runs around the centre of the Earth. It is an equal distance from the North and South Poles. Lying parallel to the Equator are lines called the Tropics of Cancer and Capricorn. Between these lines the climate and land are tropical.

North and South Poles

The North and South Poles are the most northerly and southerly points on the surface of the Earth. They are invisible and are found where all the lines of longitude meet. If you stood on the South Pole every direction would be north, and at the North Pole all directions would be south! There is no land at the North Pole, just the frozen waters of the Arctic Ocean.

North Pole

AFRICA

AFRICA

South Pole

How to use this atlas

The maps in this atlas have been arranged by continent in the following order: North America, South America, Africa, Europe, Asia, Oceania and Antarctica. Every map has a double page and the countries on each map are listed at the top left-hand side for easy reference. The Antarctic is shown with the Arctic, after all the other maps. Every map is accompanied by photographs of landscapes, wildlife, industries, famous landmarks, typical foods and interesting facts, to give you a snapshot of each area.

The indexes

This atlas has two indexes. One index gives a list of all the place names shown on the maps. The other index lists the animals, industries, and other topics in the book. To find out how to use the indexes, see p. 60.

Index to place names

Regional heading tells you which region or country the map shows.

Continent heading tells you which continent the region is in.

Introductory text sets the scene for each map, giving general information about the region.

Did you know? boxes give you some fascinating facts about the countries on each of the maps.

Locator globe shows you which region of the world the map covers.

Country index lists all the countries shown on the map.

Grid letters and numbers help you to find the cities, towns, rivers, mountains and other features listed in the index to the place names.

Photographs of animals, people and places help to bring the map to life.

Flags of each nation are shown next to their country.

Compass rose shows the direction of north for each map.

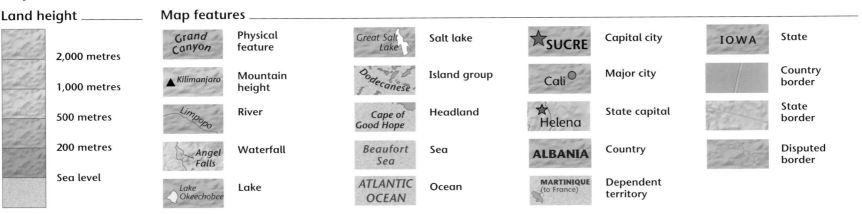

Scale bar helps you to work out the distances between places and how big countries are.

Map colours show you how high the land is.

Find out more directs you to a website where you can find more information about topics featured on the page.

Key to all the features on the maps:

Land height

- 2,000 metres
- 1,000 metres
- 500 metres
- 200 metres
- Sea level

Map features

Grand Canyon	Physical feature	*Great Salt Lake*	Salt lake
▲ *Kilimanjaro*	Mountain height	*Dodecanese*	Island group
Limpopo	River	*Cape of Good Hope*	Headland
Angel Falls	Waterfall	*Beaufort Sea*	Sea
Lake Okeechobee	Lake	*ATLANTIC OCEAN*	Ocean

☆ SUCRE	Capital city	IOWA	State
Cali ○	Major city		Country border
☆ Helena	State capital		State border
ALBANIA	Country		Disputed border
MARTINIQUE (to France)	Dependent territory		

Our planet in space

If we wrote down the address for planet Earth it would be: Earth, The Solar System, The Milky Way, The Universe. Earth belongs to the Solar System, which forms just a tiny part of the Milky Way galaxy. A galaxy is a massive group of hundreds of billions of stars. The Milky Way is one of billions of galaxies in the Universe. The Universe is the name that we give to the whole of space.

The Milky Way

Our Sun is one of 200 billion stars in the Milky Way. The Milky Way is a spiral galaxy and it is really enormous. It would take 100,000 light years to travel across it!

The Solar System

Our Solar System is made up of the Sun and the eight planets and other bodies (such as comets, moons and asteroids) that orbit around it. The Sun is a star. Its powerful gravity keeps everything orbiting around it. The four planets that are nearest to the Sun (Mercury, Venus, Earth and Mars) are made of rock and metal. The four outer planets (Jupiter, Saturn, Uranus and Neptune) are mostly gas or liquid. They are known as the gas giants.

Pluto

Pluto used to be called a planet. But in 2006 the International Astronomical Union decided that it is only a dwarf planet.

Neptune

This is the furthest planet from the Sun. A French mathematician discovered its existence in 1843 by doing calculations, but it was not actually seen for another three years.

Uranus

The blue colour of Uranus comes from the gas called methane, which is in its atmosphere. Scientists think that this planet is made of different icy materials (methane, water and ammonia) surrounding a solid core.

Saturn

This planet is surrounded by many rings. These rings are a few hundred metres thick and about 270,000 kilometres in diameter. They are formed from millions of icy particles. The ice particles range in size from tiny pieces a few millimetres across to huge lumps that are tens of metres across.

Did you know?

◈ Distances in space are measured in "light years." That is the distance that light travels in one year: 9.46 trillion kilometres!

The relative distance of the planets from the Sun

Neptune
This is about 4.5 billion km from the Sun.

Uranus

Saturn

Jupiter

Sun

Venus

Earth

Mars

Mercury

The Sun

The Sun is about 4.5 billion years old and is only half-way through its life. It is 1.4 million kilometres across and is made mostly of the gases hydrogen and helium. The temperature at its surface is 5,500°C.

The Moon
Earth's Moon is made of solid rock. It is covered in craters made by meteorites that crashed into it.

Earth
Earth is the third planet from the Sun and, as far as we know, it is the only planet in our Solar System that has any kind of life on it.

Venus
The planet Venus is the brightest object in our night sky, after the Moon. This is because its atmosphere reflects more sunlight than any other planet.

Mercury
The planet that is closest to the Sun is Mercury. This means that it has the shortest year (the time that it takes to go once round the Sun) of all the planets.

Mars
Bright red dust covers most of the planet Mars. The dust often blows into fierce sandstorms. When this happens, the surface of the planet cannot be seen.

Jupiter
This giant planet is made almost entirely of gas. Jupiter is the largest planet in the Solar System and it is 11 times larger in diameter than Earth.

Did you know?
To qualify as a planet, a body must:
1) Orbit around a sun.
2) Be big enough for its own gravity to have pulled it into a ball.
3) Have cleared other bodies out of its orbit.

Planet Earth's many layers

The rocky layer of Earth that we live on is called the crust. It is about 40 kilometres thick. Scientists believe that the inner core of Earth is solid iron. This is surrounded by a molten layer of iron and nickel, which is called the outer core. Between Earth's outer core and its crust is the mantle.

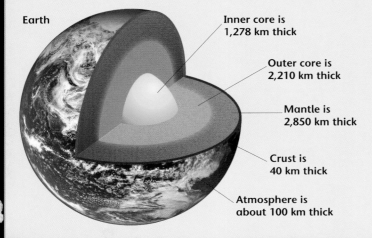

Earth

Inner core is 1,278 km thick

Outer core is 2,210 km thick

Mantle is 2,850 km thick

Crust is 40 km thick

Atmosphere is about 100 km thick

When the surface of the Earth moves

Earth's crust is made up of tectonic plates, which are constantly moving and pushing past each other. Most of the time the movements are so small that we do not notice them. But sometimes, during an earthquake or a volcanic eruption, the Earth moves violently and these movements are easy to notice.

Earthquake
When tectonic plates stick together instead of sliding past each other, stress builds up in the rocks until they crack or "fault." This cracking sends shock waves through the Earth, causing an earthquake. Powerful earthquakes can sometimes destroy whole cities.

Volcano
Where the Earth's crust is weak, or at the point between two tectonic plates, magma (molten rock) seeps out and volcanoes can develop over time. The pressure of magma pushing up to the Earth's surface can be so powerful that a volcano will erupt, spewing out lava.

Physical features of the world

Greenland

Greenland Sea

Spitsbergen

Franz Josef Land

Severnaya Zemlya

New Siberian Islands

Novaya Zemlya

Kara Sea

Taymyr Peninsula

Laptev Sea

Barents Sea

North Siberian Lowland

Norwegian Sea

Pechora

Ob'

Central Siberian Plateau

Lena

Verkhoyanskiy Khrebet

Arctic Circle

Denmark Strait

Iceland

Faeroe Islands

Scandinavia

Northern Dvina

Lake Onega

West Siberian Plain

Siberia

Yenisey

Ural Mountains

North Sea

Lake Ladoga

Baltic Sea

North European Plain

Volga

Ob'

Irtysh

Angara

Lena

Aldan

Sea of Okhotsk

Ireland

Great Britain

EUROPE

Dnieper

Yenisey

Lake Baikal

Amur

Sakhalin

ATLANTIC OCEAN

Bay of Biscay

Rhine

Loire

Alps

Carpathian Mountains

Don

Volga

Lake Balkhash

Altai Mountains

ASIA

Manchurian Plain

Kuril Islands

Danube

Black Sea

Caucasus

El'brus 5642m

Caspian Sea

Aral Sea

Tien Shan

Gobi

Sea of Japan

Hokkaido

Iberian Peninsula

Azores

Mediterranean Sea

Anatolia

Amu Darya

Takla Makan Desert

Yellow River

Great Plain of China

Yellow Sea

Honshu

Atlas Mountains

Zagros Mountains

Tigris

Euphrates

Iranian Plateau

Hindu Kush

Himalayas

Plateau of Tibet

Brahmaputra

Mount Everest 8850m

Yangtze

East China Sea

Shikoku

Kyushu

Tropic of Cancer

Canary Islands

Libyan Desert

The Gulf

Indus

Thar Desert

Ganges

Deccan

Xi Jiang

Taiwan

Sahara Desert

Nile

Red Sea

Arabian Peninsula

Arabian Sea

Bay of Bengal

Irrawaddy

Salween

Mekong

Philippine Sea

Mariana Islands

Cape Verde Islands

Senegal

Niger

Sahel

Lake Chad

White Nile

Blue Nile

Gulf of Aden

Laccadive Islands

Andaman Islands

South China Sea

Phillipine Islands

Micronesia

AFRICA

Ethiopian Highlands

Nicobar Islands

Malay Peninsula

Celebes Sea

Caroline Islands

Gulf of Guinea

Ubangi

Great Rift Valley

Maldive Islands

Sri Lanka

Sumatra

Borneo

Sulawesi

New Guinea

Equator

Congo

Congo Basin

Great Rift Valley

Lake Victoria

Kilimanjaro 5895m

Java Sea

East Indies

Java

Ascension Island

Lake Tanganyika

Seychelles

Chagos Archipelago

Timor

Arafura Sea

St Helena

Lake Nyasa

Comoros Islands

Cocos Islands

Coral Sea

Zambezi

Mozambique Channel

Madagascar

Mauritius

Réunion

INDIAN OCEAN

Great Sandy Desert

Simpson Desert

Great Dividing Range

Tropic of Capricorn

Namib Desert

Kalahari Desert

AUSTRALIA

ATLANTIC OCEAN

Orange River

Nullarbor Plain

Darling

Cape of Good Hope

Great Australian Bight

Mount Kosciuszko 2228m

Tasmania

Prince Edward Islands

Crozet Islands

Kerguelen

SOUTHERN OCEAN

Antarctic Circle

ANTARCTICA

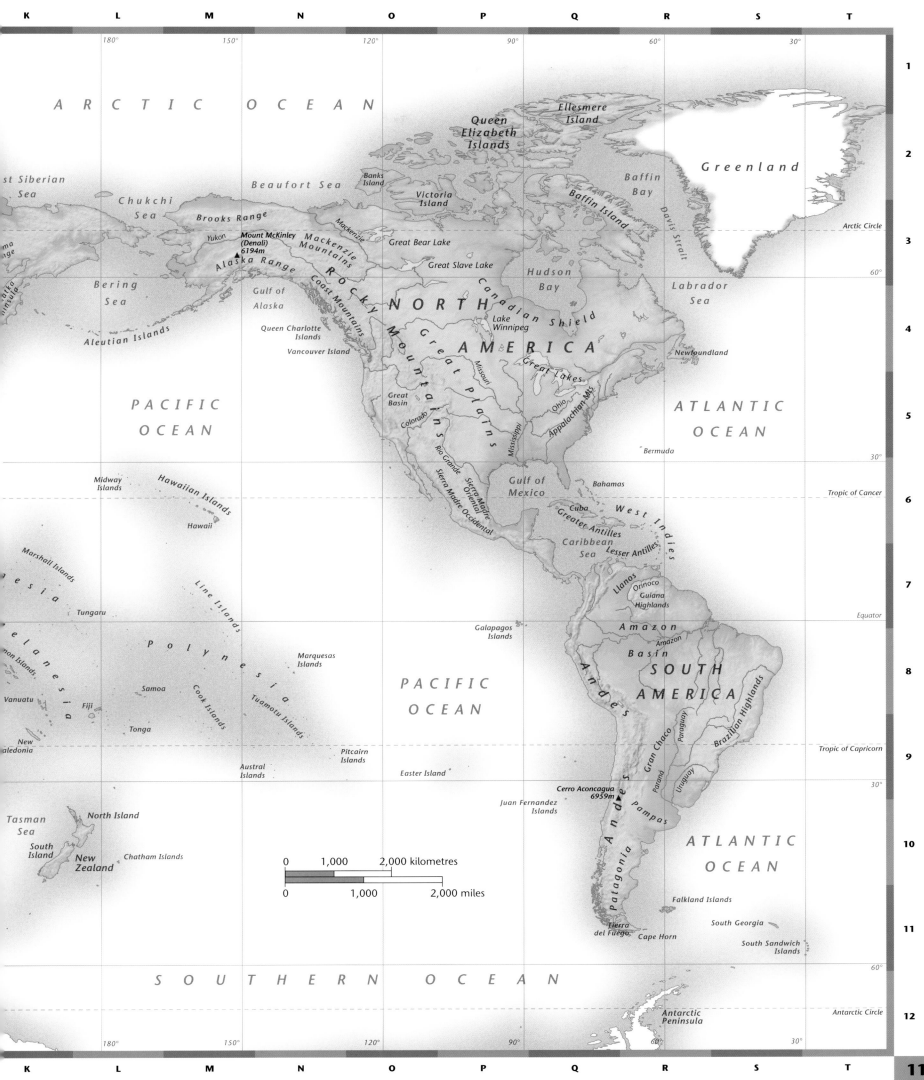

1

A R C T I C   O C E A N

Queen
Elizabeth
Islands

Ellesmere
Island

Greenland

2

*st Siberian
Sea*

*Chukchi
Sea*

Beaufort Sea

Banks
Island

Baffin
Bay

Arctic Circle

3

Brooks Range

Victoria
Island

Baffin Island

Davis Strait

*ma
nge*

Yukon

Mount McKinley
(Denali)
6194m

Mackenzie
Mountains

Mackenzie

Great Bear Lake

60°

*ka
insula*

Alaska Range

Great Slave Lake

Hudson
Bay

Labrador
Sea

4

*Bering
Sea*

Gulf of
Alaska

Coast Mountains

N O R T H

Canadian Shield

Aleutian Islands

Queen Charlotte
Islands

Rocky Mountains

Lake
Winnipeg

Newfoundland

Vancouver Island

A M E R I C A

Great Lakes

5

P A C I F I C

OCEAN

Great
Basin

Great Plains

Missouri

Ohio

Appalachian Mts.

A T L A N T I C

OCEAN

Colorado

Mississippi

Rio Grande

Bermuda

30°

*Midway
Islands*

Hawaiian Islands

Sierra Madre Occidental

Sierra Madre
Oriental

Gulf of
Mexico

Bahamas

Tropic of Cancer

6

Hawaii

Cuba

West Indies

Greater Antilles

Caribbean
Sea

Lesser Antilles

Marshall Islands

Llanos

Orinoco

Guiana
Highlands

7

nesia

Line Islands

A m a z o n

Equator

elanesia

mon Islands

P o l y n e s i a

Galapagos
Islands

Basin

Amazon

8

Vanuatu

Samoa

Cook Islands

Marquesas
Islands

P A C I F I C

S O U T H

Fiji

Tuamotu Islands

OCEAN

A M E R I C A

Andes

*New
aledonia*

Tonga

Gran Chaco

Paraguay

Brazilian Highlands

Pitcairn
Islands

Tropic of Capricorn

9

*Austral
Islands*

Easter Island

Paraná

Uruguay

Cerro Aconcagua
6959m

Juan Fernandez
Islands

30°

*Tasman
Sea*

North Island

Andes

Pampas

10

*South
Island*

Chatham Islands

0   1,000   2,000 kilometres

A T L A N T I C

New
Zealand

0   1,000   2,000 miles

OCEAN

Patagonia

Falkland Islands

South Georgia

11

*Tierra
del Fuego*

Cape Horn

South Sandwich
Islands

60°

S O U T H E R N   O C E A N

12

Antarctic Circle

Antarctic
Peninsula

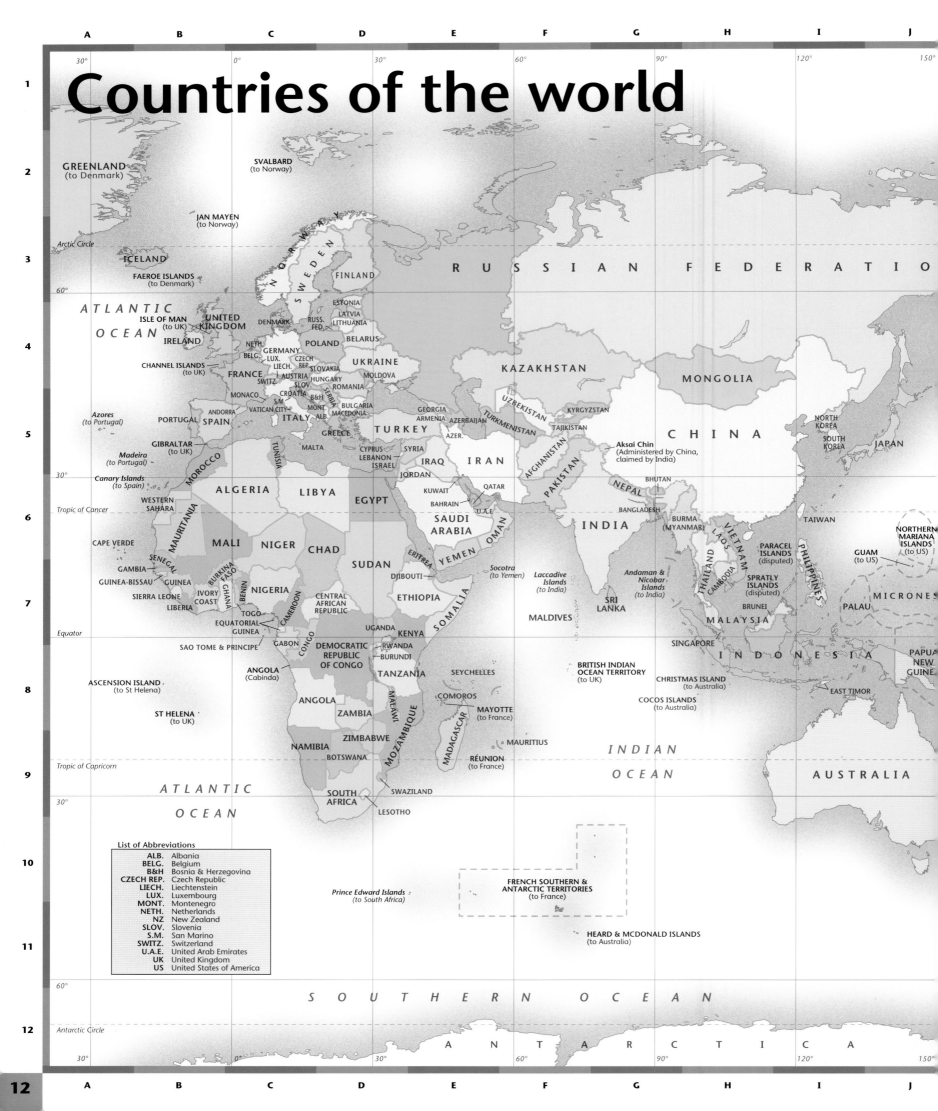

Countries of the world

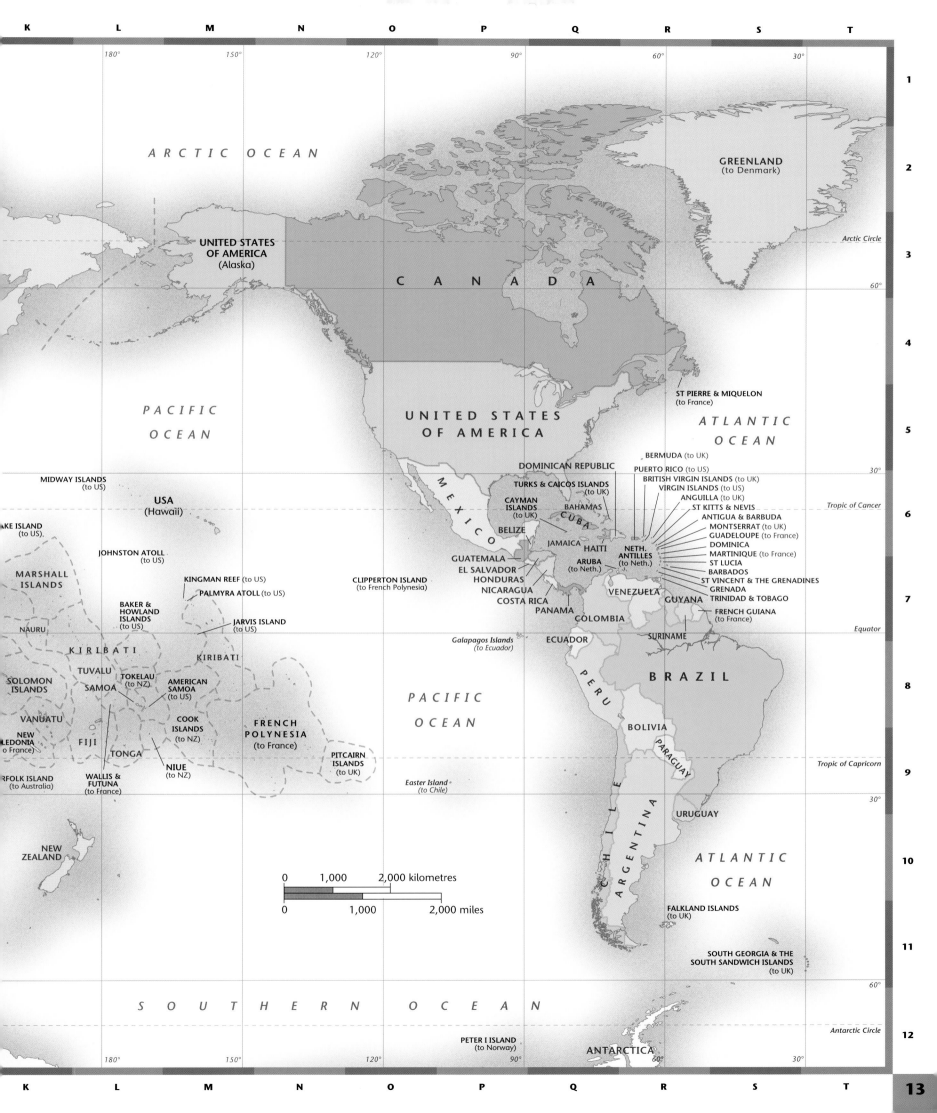

180°   150°   120°   90°   60°   30°

1

ARCTIC OCEAN

GREENLAND
(to Denmark)

2

Arctic Circle

UNITED STATES
OF AMERICA
(Alaska)

C A N A D A

60°

3

4

PACIFIC

OCEAN

ST PIERRE & MIQUELON
(to France)

ATLANTIC

OCEAN

5

UNITED STATES
OF AMERICA

BERMUDA (to UK)

30°

MIDWAY ISLANDS
(to US)

DOMINICAN REPUBLIC

PUERTO RICO (to US)
BRITISH VIRGIN ISLANDS (to UK)
VIRGIN ISLANDS (to US)
ANGUILLA (to UK)
ST KITTS & NEVIS

Tropic of Cancer

6

USA
(Hawaii)

TURKS & CAICOS ISLANDS
(to UK)

CAYMAN
ISLANDS
(to UK)

BAHAMAS

CUBA

ANTIGUA & BARBUDA
MONTSERRAT (to UK)
GUADELOUPE (to France)
DOMINICA
MARTINIQUE (to France)
ST LUCIA
BARBADOS
ST VINCENT & THE GRENADINES
GRENADA
TRINIDAD & TOBAGO

KE ISLAND
(to US)

MEXICO

BELIZE

JAMAICA

HAITI

NETH.
ANTILLES
(to Neth.)

JOHNSTON ATOLL
(to US)

GUATEMALA
EL SALVADOR
HONDURAS
NICARAGUA
COSTA RICA

ARUBA
(to Neth.)

MARSHALL
ISLANDS

KINGMAN REEF (to US)

PALMYRA ATOLL (to US)

CLIPPERTON ISLAND
(to French Polynesia)

VENEZUELA

GUYANA

FRENCH GUIANA
(to France)

7

BAKER &
HOWLAND
ISLANDS
(to US)

JARVIS ISLAND
(to US)

PANAMA

COLOMBIA

NAURU

SURINAME

Equator

Galapagos Islands
(to Ecuador)

ECUADOR

KIRIBATI

KIRIBATI

B R A Z I L

TUVALU

PERU

8

SOLOMON
ISLANDS

SAMOA

TOKELAU
(to NZ)

AMERICAN
SAMOA
(to US)

PACIFIC

OCEAN

VANUATU

COOK
ISLANDS
(to NZ)

BOLIVIA

NEW
EDONIA
o France)

FIJI

TONGA

FRENCH
POLYNESIA
(to France)

PARAGUAY

RFOLK ISLAND
(to Australia)

WALLIS &
FUTUNA
(to France)

NIUE
(to NZ)

PITCAIRN
ISLANDS
(to UK)

CHILE

ARGENTINA

Tropic of Capricorn

9

Easter Island
(to Chile)

30°

URUGUAY

NEW
ZEALAND

0   1,000   2,000 kilometres

ATLANTIC

OCEAN

10

0   1,000   2,000 miles

FALKLAND ISLANDS
(to UK)

11

SOUTH GEORGIA & THE
SOUTH SANDWICH ISLANDS
(to UK)

60°

S O U T H E R N   O C E A N

12

Antarctic Circle

PETER I ISLAND
(to Norway)

ANTARCTICA

180°   150°   120°   90°   60°   30°

Climate and land cover

Climate is the average pattern of the weather over about 30 years. The climate of a place depends on how much sunshine and rain it gets, how close it is to the sea and sea currents, and how high it is above sea level. Different kinds of plants grow in different climates. The type of vegetation in an area, such as grassland or tropical forest, is called "land cover." Different land cover is suitable for different animals. The countries around the Equator get the most sunlight and rain. It is there that the habitats with the largest numbers of animals and plants are found. In places where there is little rainfall or the temperatures are too hot or cold, such as the Sahara or the North and South Poles, only a few species of plants and animals are able to survive.

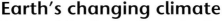

■ Temperate broadleaf forest

Forests in temperate parts of the world have mild temperatures and plenty of rain. These forests contain trees such as oak, beech, birch and chestnut. Broadleaved trees collect nutrients in summer and shed their leaves in autumn to save energy and water.

■ Tropical broadleaf forest

Tropical forests that grow near the Equator have high temperatures and receive heavy rainfall all year round. These forests may contain over 50,000 different species of trees, as well as huge numbers of other plants and animals.

Earth's changing climate

The world's climate is gradually changing, and this is having huge effects on its wildlife and people. Some areas have unusual floods and other places are affected by drought. Many kinds of animals, including polar bears, are threatened by climate change. Not all the animals and plants will be able to adapt to these new conditions.

Did you know?

◈ The different environments (habitats) on planet Earth where life exists are called biomes. A certain area, such as a forest or desert, is called an ecosystem.

Extreme weather

Violent storms, heavy rainfall, strong winds and long periods of sunshine are all examples of extreme weather. Extreme weather often causes widespread flooding or drought, and the effects of these can be devastating. People may be killed or left homeless, and crops, farm animals and wildlife may be destroyed.

Needleleaf forest

Stretching across northern parts of Asia, Europe and North America is a belt of tall, evergreen trees with needle-like leaves. They can survive cold winters because they gather nutrients all year.

Cropland

Many of the most fertile areas of the world, especially Europe and North America, do not have their natural land cover. This has been cleared over hundreds of years to grow crops for food.

Grassland

In areas of a continent where there is not enough rain for trees to grow, there are huge grasslands. These are called steppes and prairies in the north. In South America they are known as pampas.

Tundra

Areas of tundra are mostly found near the Arctic Circle. The soil is frozen for much of the year. In places where it melts for a few months, plants such as lichens, mosses and low shrubs are able to grow.

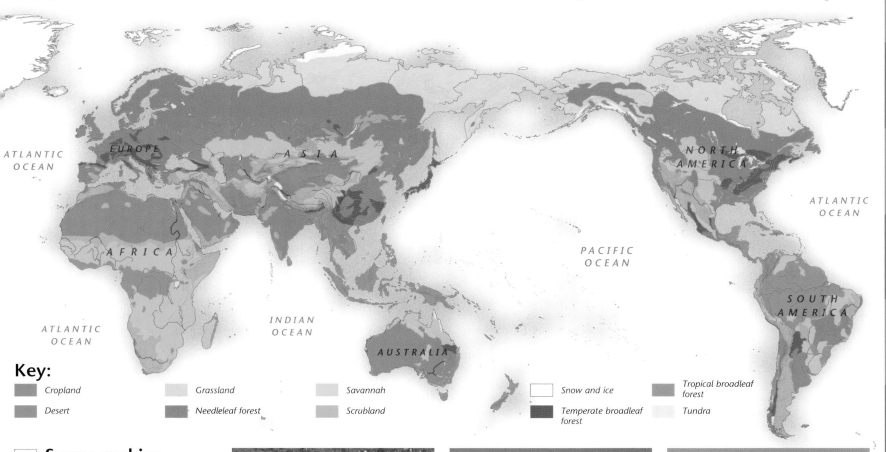

ATLANTIC OCEAN

EUROPE

ASIA

NORTH AMERICA

ATLANTIC OCEAN

AFRICA

PACIFIC OCEAN

ATLANTIC OCEAN

INDIAN OCEAN

SOUTH AMERICA

AUSTRALIA

Key:

Cropland	Grassland	Savannah
Desert	Needleleaf forest	Scrubland

Snow and ice

Temperate broadleaf forest

Tropical broadleaf forest

Tundra

Snow and ice

In the Arctic and Antarctic, and on the highest parts of mountain ranges, such as the Alps and the Andes, there is snow and ice all year round. Temperatures remain well below freezing and it is often windy. Very few animals and plants can survive in such a harsh environment.

Scrubland

At the edges of both hot and cold deserts there are areas of scrubland. Where it is too hot or too cold for trees to survive, tough, spiny shrubs with small leaves grow well.

Desert

Deserts have very little water and are often windy. Few plants or animals can survive, as temperatures soar to over 40°C in the day and drop to below freezing at night.

Savannah

Between hot deserts and tropical forests are areas called savannah. There is grass here and lots of trees, but the trees do not grow close together in big groups.

15

Planet Earth's population

Every second, the world's population gets larger by two or three people. Scientists say that the world's population will reach 9 billion in 2050, at today's rates of births and deaths. People live in most parts of the world, but they are not evenly distributed. Some countries, such as Singapore, have dense populations with thousands of people for every square kilometre of land (which is called its population density), but others, such as Mongolia, have fewer than two people for every square kilometre. Most of the areas where hardly any people live are either too hot and dry, such as the Sahara, or too cold, such as the poles.

Is there enough for everyone?

As the world's population continues to grow, more houses, food, water and fuel are needed. In some areas there is not enough clean water or shelter for everyone. Some countries cannot grow enough food, and do not have enough fuel supplies.

World population

This map shows how the world's population is spread out. Most people live in South and East Asia. In 1900 only a few towns had more than 1 million people living in them. Now 25 of the world's cities have over 15 million people.

EUROPE has mostly warm summers and mild winters, and much of the land is fertile and easy to farm, which provides ideal living conditions.

AFRICA has the Sahara, which is the biggest desert in the world. Living here is difficult because the temperatures range from 50°C during the day to below 0°C at night. Most people living here belong to nomadic tribes.

RUSSIAN FEDERATION

ATLANTIC OCEAN

EUROPE

ASIA

Cairo

Karachi

Delhi

Seoul
Tokyo
Osaka
Shanghai

Mumbai

Kolkata

Manila

AFRICA

SOUTH ASIA has the biggest, and one of the fastest-growing populations in the world. One-fifth of the world's population lives in this area.

Jakarta

AUSTRALIA

INDIAN OCEAN

Busy, busy cities

In the 1900s, only 1 out of every 10 people lived in a city. Now more than 5 out of 10 people live in cities. India and China have the most cities with over one million people, even though two-thirds of their populations live in the countryside. By 2030 almost two-thirds of the world's population may live in cities.

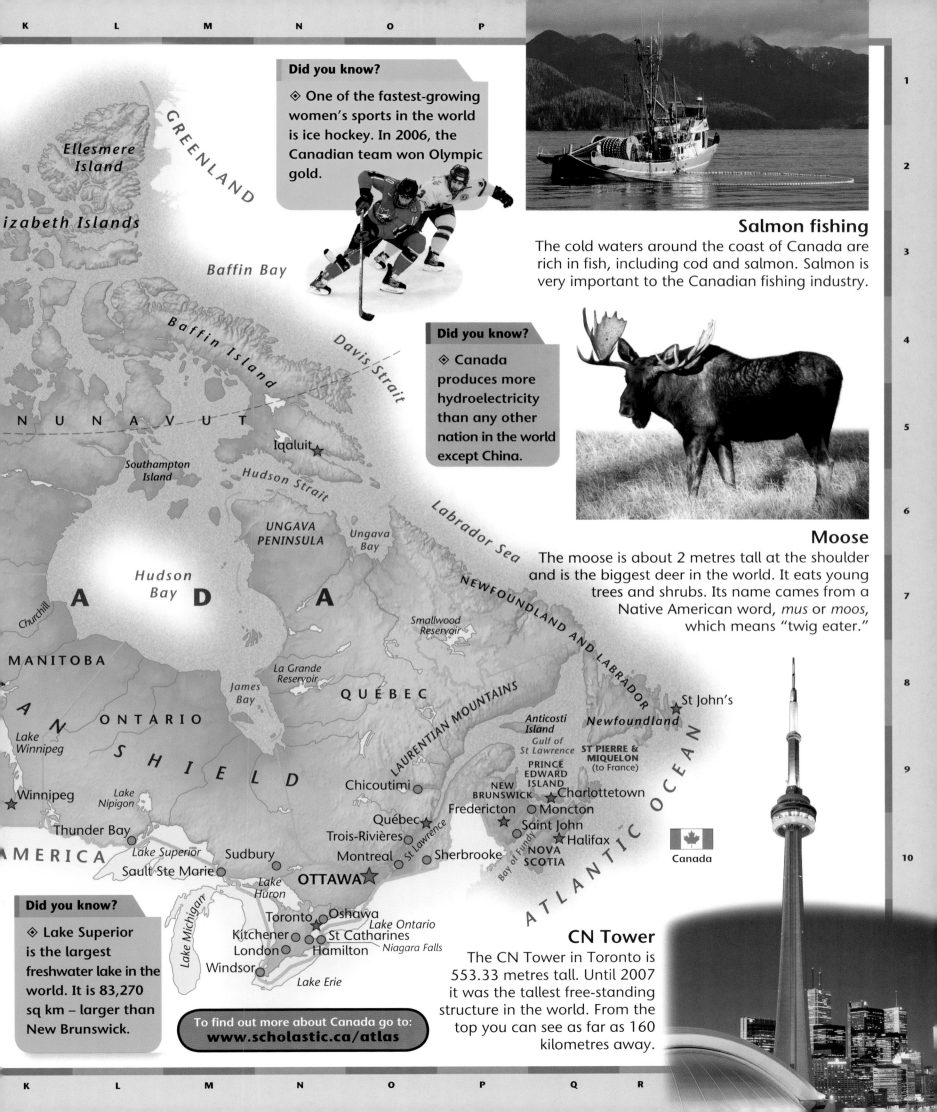

Did you know?

◈ One of the fastest-growing women's sports in the world is ice hockey. In 2006, the Canadian team won Olympic gold.

Salmon fishing

The cold waters around the coast of Canada are rich in fish, including cod and salmon. Salmon is very important to the Canadian fishing industry.

Did you know?

◈ Canada produces more hydroelectricity than any other nation in the world except China.

Moose

The moose is about 2 metres tall at the shoulder and is the biggest deer in the world. It eats young trees and shrubs. Its name cames from a Native American word, *mus* or *moos*, which means "twig eater."

GREENLAND

Ellesmere Island

izabeth Islands

Baffin Bay

Baffin Island

Davis Strait

N U N A V U T

Iqaluit ☆

Southampton Island

Hudson Strait

Labrador Sea

UNGAVA PENINSULA

Ungava Bay

Hudson Bay

A   D   A

NEWFOUNDLAND AND LABRADOR

Churchill

Smallwood Reservoir

MANITOBA

La Grande Reservoir

James Bay

QUÉBEC

St John's ☆

A   N

ONTARIO

LAURENTIAN MOUNTAINS

Anticosti Island

Newfoundland

Lake Winnipeg

Gulf of St Lawrence

ST PIERRE & MIQUELON (to France)

S   H   I   E   L   D

PRINCE EDWARD ISLAND

Winnipeg ☆

Lake Nipigon

Chicoutimi ○

NEW BRUNSWICK

Charlottetown ☆

Thunder Bay ○

Québec ☆

Fredericton ○ Moncton

St Lawrence

Saint John ☆

A M E R I C A

Lake Superior

Sudbury ○

Trois-Rivières

Montreal ○

Sherbrooke ○

Halifax ☆

NOVA SCOTIA

Sault Ste Marie ○

Lake Huron

OTTAWA ☆

Bay of Fundy

A T L A N T I C   O C E A N

🍁
Canada

Did you know?

◈ Lake Superior is the largest freshwater lake in the world. It is 83,270 sq km – larger than New Brunswick.

Lake Michigan

Toronto ○ Oshawa

Kitchener ○ St Catharines

London ○ Hamilton

Lake Ontario

Niagara Falls

Windsor ○

Lake Erie

CN Tower

The CN Tower in Toronto is 553.33 metres tall. Until 2007 it was the tallest free-standing structure in the world. From the top you can see as far as 160 kilometres away.

To find out more about Canada go to:
www.scholastic.ca/atlas

United States of America
NORTH AMERICA

The United States of America (USA) covers an area almost the size of Europe. It includes the states of Alaska at the northwest tip of Canada, and Hawaii in the Pacific Ocean. The land and climate of the USA change dramatically across this huge area. There are deserts, mountains, prairies and swamps. In Alaska temperatures drop to below −30°C in winter. In the southeast the temperature rarely drops below 10°C. The population of over 301 million contains people descended from immigrants from all over the world, especially Europe. There are also 2.4 million Native American people. The USA is one of the world's wealthiest nations. There are huge oil and gas fields in Texas and Oklahoma, minerals are mined in Montana and Wyoming, and California is a centre for the computer industry.

Country File

United States of America

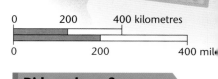

Detroit has been home to the USA's motor industry since Henry Ford built his first vehicle there in 1896.

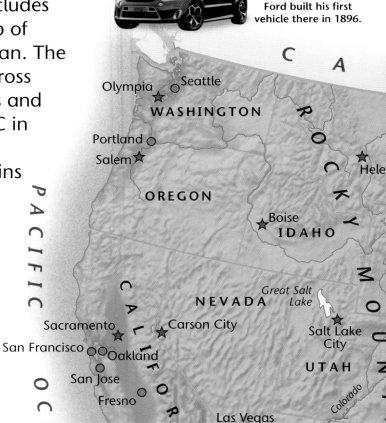

The sunny state of California produces half of the USA's fruit and vegetables.

Monument Valley
The great "buttes" of Monument Valley, on the border of Utah and Arizona, were formed by rivers, rain and wind, which have eroded the soft rock around them over millions of years. The land between the buttes was once as high as they are. Their red colour comes from iron oxide in the soil, which is also known as rust.

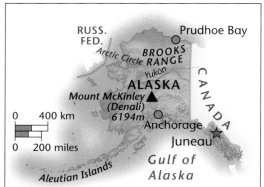

Did you know?

◈ The 16 highest mountains in the United States of America are all in Alaska. The highest is Mount McKinley.

Did you know?

◈ The Grand Canyon in Arizona is one of the natural wonders of the world.

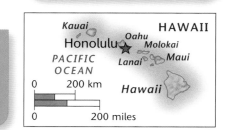

Did you know?

◈ The border between the USA and Canada is the longest in the world. It measures 8,893 km, including the border with Alaska.

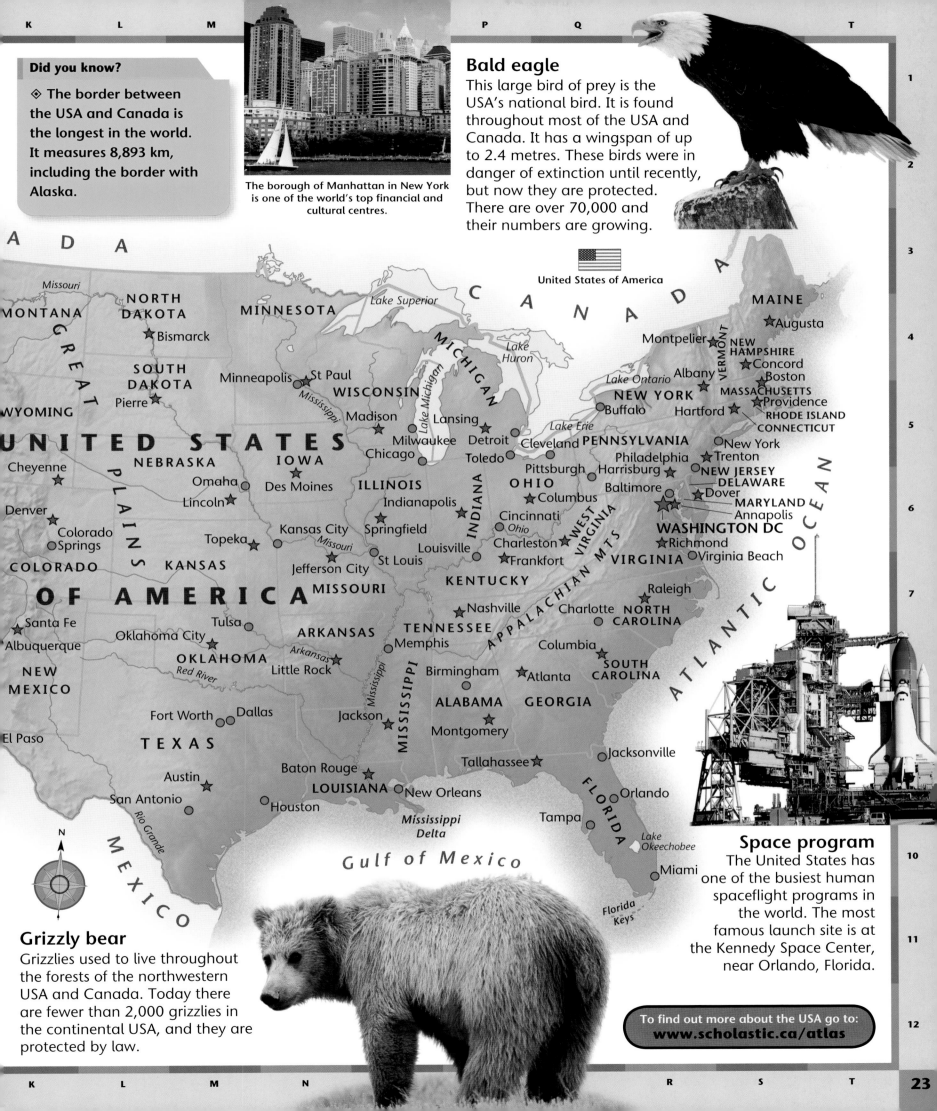

The borough of Manhattan in New York is one of the world's top financial and cultural centres.

Bald eagle
This large bird of prey is the USA's national bird. It is found throughout most of the USA and Canada. It has a wingspan of up to 2.4 metres. These birds were in danger of extinction until recently, but now they are protected. There are over 70,000 and their numbers are growing.

United States of America

C A N A D A

A D A

MONTANA

NORTH DAKOTA
☆ Bismarck

MINNESOTA

Lake Superior

Missouri

MICHIGAN

Lake Huron

MAINE
☆ Augusta

Montpelier ☆
VERMONT
NEW HAMPSHIRE
☆ Concord

SOUTH DAKOTA
Pierre ☆

Minneapolis St Paul ☆
WISCONSIN
Mississippi

Lake Michigan

Lake Ontario Albany ☆
Boston ☆
MASSACHUSETTS
☆ Providence
RHODE ISLAND
CONNECTICUT

WYOMING

Madison
Milwaukee
Chicago
Lansing ☆
Detroit
Cleveland
Toledo

Lake Erie

NEW YORK
Buffalo ○
Hartford ☆

PENNSYLVANIA
Philadelphia ○ New York
Trenton ☆
NEW JERSEY
DELAWARE

G R E A T

U N I T E D   S T A T E S

Cheyenne ☆

NEBRASKA

IOWA

ILLINOIS

OHIO

Pittsburgh Harrisburg ☆
☆ Columbus
Cincinnati ○ Ohio

WEST VIRGINIA

Baltimore ○
Dover ○
MARYLAND
Annapolis

P L A I N S

Omaha ○
Lincoln ☆
Des Moines ☆

Indianapolis ☆

INDIANA

WASHINGTON DC

Denver ☆
Colorado ○ Springs

Topeka ☆ ○
Kansas City

Springfield ☆

Louisville

Charleston ☆
Frankfort ☆

VIRGINIA
☆ Richmond
Virginia Beach ○

COLORADO

KANSAS

Missouri

St Louis ○

KENTUCKY

O F   A M E R I C A

Jefferson City ☆
MISSOURI

APPALACHIAN MTS

Raleigh ☆

Santa Fe ☆

Tulsa ○

Nashville ☆

Charlotte ○
NORTH CAROLINA

Albuquerque ☆

Oklahoma City ☆
OKLAHOMA
Little Rock ☆

ARKANSAS

Arkansas
Red River

TENNESSEE

Memphis ○

Columbia ☆
SOUTH CAROLINA

NEW MEXICO

El Paso ○

Fort Worth ○ ○ Dallas

TEXAS

Jackson ☆

MISSISSIPPI

Birmingham ○
☆ Atlanta

ALABAMA
GEORGIA

Montgomery ☆

Jacksonville ○

Austin ☆
San Antonio ○

Baton Rouge ☆
LOUISIANA ○ New Orleans
Houston ○

Tallahassee ☆

FLORIDA

Orlando ○

Rio Grande

M E X I C O

Mississippi Delta

Gulf of Mexico

Tampa ○

Lake Okeechobee

Miami ○

Florida Keys

N

Grizzly bear
Grizzlies used to live throughout the forests of the northwestern USA and Canada. Today there are fewer than 2,000 grizzlies in the continental USA, and they are protected by law.

Space program
The United States has one of the busiest human spaceflight programs in the world. The most famous launch site is at the Kennedy Space Center, near Orlando, Florida.

To find out more about the USA go to:
www.scholastic.ca/atlas

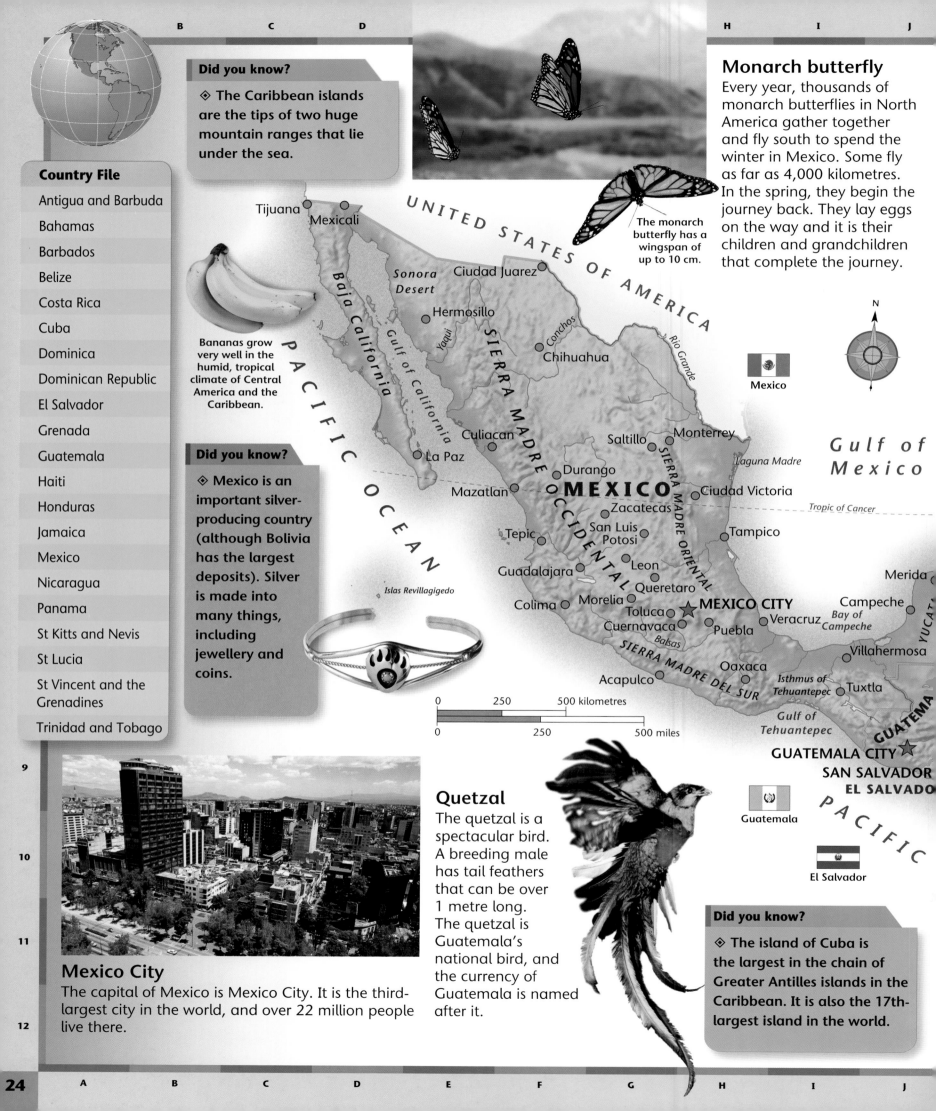

Monarch butterfly

Every year, thousands of monarch butterflies in North America gather together and fly south to spend the winter in Mexico. Some fly as far as 4,000 kilometres. In the spring, they begin the journey back. They lay eggs on the way and it is their children and grandchildren that complete the journey.

The monarch butterfly has a wingspan of up to 10 cm.

Country File

Antigua and Barbuda

Bahamas

Barbados

Belize

Costa Rica

Cuba

Dominica

Dominican Republic

El Salvador

Grenada

Guatemala

Haiti

Honduras

Jamaica

Mexico

Nicaragua

Panama

St Kitts and Nevis

St Lucia

St Vincent and the Grenadines

Trinidad and Tobago

Bananas grow very well in the humid, tropical climate of Central America and the Caribbean.

Did you know?

◈ Mexico is an important silver-producing country (although Bolivia has the largest deposits). Silver is made into many things, including jewellery and coins.

UNITED STATES OF AMERICA

Tijuana
Mexicali
Baja California
Sonora Desert
Ciudad Juarez
Hermosillo
Yaqui
Conchos
Chihuahua
Rio Grande
Gulf of California
SIERRA MADRE OCCIDENTAL
Culiacan
La Paz
Saltillo
Monterrey
Laguna Madre
Durango
MEXICO
Ciudad Victoria
SIERRA MADRE ORIENTAL
Mazatlan
Zacatecas
Tropic of Cancer
Tepic
San Luis Potosi
Tampico
Islas Revillagigedo
Guadalajara
Leon
Queretaro
Merida
Colima
Morelia
MEXICO CITY
Campeche
Toluca
Veracruz
Bay of Campeche
Cuernavaca
Puebla
YUCAT
Balsas
Villahermosa
SIERRA MADRE DEL SUR
Oaxaca
Acapulco
Isthmus of Tehuantepec
Tuxtla
Gulf of Tehuantepec
GUATE

Gulf of Mexico

Mexico

N

PACIFIC OCEAN

0 — 250 — 500 kilometres
0 — 250 — 500 miles

GUATEMALA CITY
SAN SALVADOR
EL SALVADO

Guatemala

PACIFIC

El Salvador

Quetzal

The quetzal is a spectacular bird. A breeding male has tail feathers that can be over 1 metre long. The quetzal is Guatemala's national bird, and the currency of Guatemala is named after it.

Mexico City

The capital of Mexico is Mexico City. It is the third-largest city in the world, and over 22 million people live there.

Central America and the Caribbean
NORTH AMERICA

The continents of North and South America are linked by Central America. To the east are the Greater and Lesser Antilles islands, which are also known as the Caribbean islands. All along Central America there are mountains and volcanoes. In the north there are hot, dry deserts and in the south there are tropical rainforests. The Caribbean also has rainforests and a tropical climate. Most of the people who live in this region are descended from Africans, Asians and Europeans. In Central America, fishing, coffee and fruit-growing are important industries. Most of Mexico's income comes from oil and gas. Tourism and sugar farming are important in the Caribbean.

Caribbean islands
The islands of the Caribbean are popular holiday destinations. Many tourists are attracted by the warm, clear sea, sandy beaches and tropical climate.

Bahamas

Cuba

NASSAU

Andros Island

BAHAMAS

ATLANTIC OCEAN

HAVANA

Matanzas

Pinar del Rio

CUBA

Camaguey

TURKS & CAICOS ISLANDS
(to UK)

GUANTANAMO BAY
(to US)

Hispaniola

Santiago de Cuba

CAYMAN ISLANDS
(to UK)

Cancun

Isla Cozumel

Greater

HAITI

PORT-AU-PRINCE

DOMINICAN REPUBLIC

SANTO DOMINGO

Belize

JAMAICA

KINGSTON

Antilles

VIRGIN ISLANDS
(to US)

BRITISH VIRGIN ISLANDS
(to UK)

PUERTO RICO
(to US)

SAN JUAN

ANGUILLA
(to UK)

Leeward Islands

Antigua and Barbuda

ANTIGUA & BARBUDA

ST KITTS & NEVIS

MONTSERRAT
(to UK)

GUADELOUPE
(to France)

DOMINICA

MARTINIQUE
(to France)

Dominica

Belize City

BELMOPAN
BELIZE

Honduras

Jamaica

Haiti

Dominican Republic

St Kitts and Nevis

St Lucia

Barbados

HONDURAS

TEGUCIGALPA

Caribbean Sea

ARUBA
(to Netherlands)

NETHERLANDS ANTILLES
(to Netherlands)

Lesser Antilles

Windward Islands

ST LUCIA

BARBADOS

ST VINCENT & THE GRENADINES

GRENADA

Tobago

TRINIDAD & TOBAGO

St Vincent and the Grenadines

NICARAGUA

MANAGUA

Leon

Lake Nicaragua

Nicaragua

Panama

COLOMBIA

VENEZUELA

Trinidad and Tobago

Grenada

SAN JOSE

Limon

Colon

Panama Canal

Gulf of Darien

PANAMA CITY

COSTA RICA

PANAMA

OCEAN

Costa Rica

Panama Canal
The Pacific and Atlantic Oceans are linked by the Panama Canal. This waterway is about 80 kilometres long. By using the canal, a boat travelling from one coast of North America to the other can avoid going around Cape Horn in South America and cut its journey by about 15,000 kilometres.

To find out more about Central America and the Caribbean go to:
www.scholastic.ca/atlas

South America
SOUTH AMERICA

The continent of South America is home to the Amazon rainforest and mountains of the Andes. The Amazon River is about 6,500 kilometres long and is the greatest river in South America. The climate ranges from tropical in the north to bitterly cold in the south – the tip of South America is only 1,000 kilometres away from Antarctica. In between, the climate is less extreme. There are wide, open grasslands called the pampas, where cattle and cereals are farmed. Northern South America is rich in oil and gas, especially in Venezuela. Further south, copper and iron ore are found. Coffee is the most important crop in South America, and Brazil is the world's leading coffee grower. Cocoa, sugar cane and bananas are also important crops.

Country File
- Argentina
- Bolivia
- Brazil
- Chile
- Colombia
- Ecuador
- Guyana
- Paraguay
- Peru
- Suriname
- Uruguay
- Venezuela

6

Angel Falls
The highest waterfall in the world is Angel Falls in Venezuela. Angel Falls is almost 1 kilometre high – 19 times higher than Niagara Falls.

Did you know?

◈ Bolivia has two capital cities – La Paz and Sucre. La Paz is 3,600 m above sea level, which makes it the highest capital city in the world.

◈ Ecuador exports more bananas than any other country in the world.

Many vegetables, such as tomatoes, potatoes, beans and corn, originally came from South America.

Carnival time
Every year, just before Lent, Carnival begins in Rio de Janeiro, Brazil. For five days people dress up, dance and parade through the streets to the sound of samba music. There is a competition for the most outrageous costume and the best-decorated float.

10

Amazon rainforest
The Amazon rainforest is the largest tropical rainforest in the world. Many scientists believe that more than one-third of all the world's species of plants and animals live there. About 1.5 square kilometres of Brazilian rainforest are destroyed every hour, as the forest is cut down for timber and cleared for farming. If this continues, the rainforest will eventually be gone. Hundreds of thousands of species of animals and plants will be lost forever.

11

12

Jaguar
For its size, the jaguar is one of the strongest mammals in the world. This cat can kill prey over three times its own body weight. It is good at climbing, crawling and swimming.

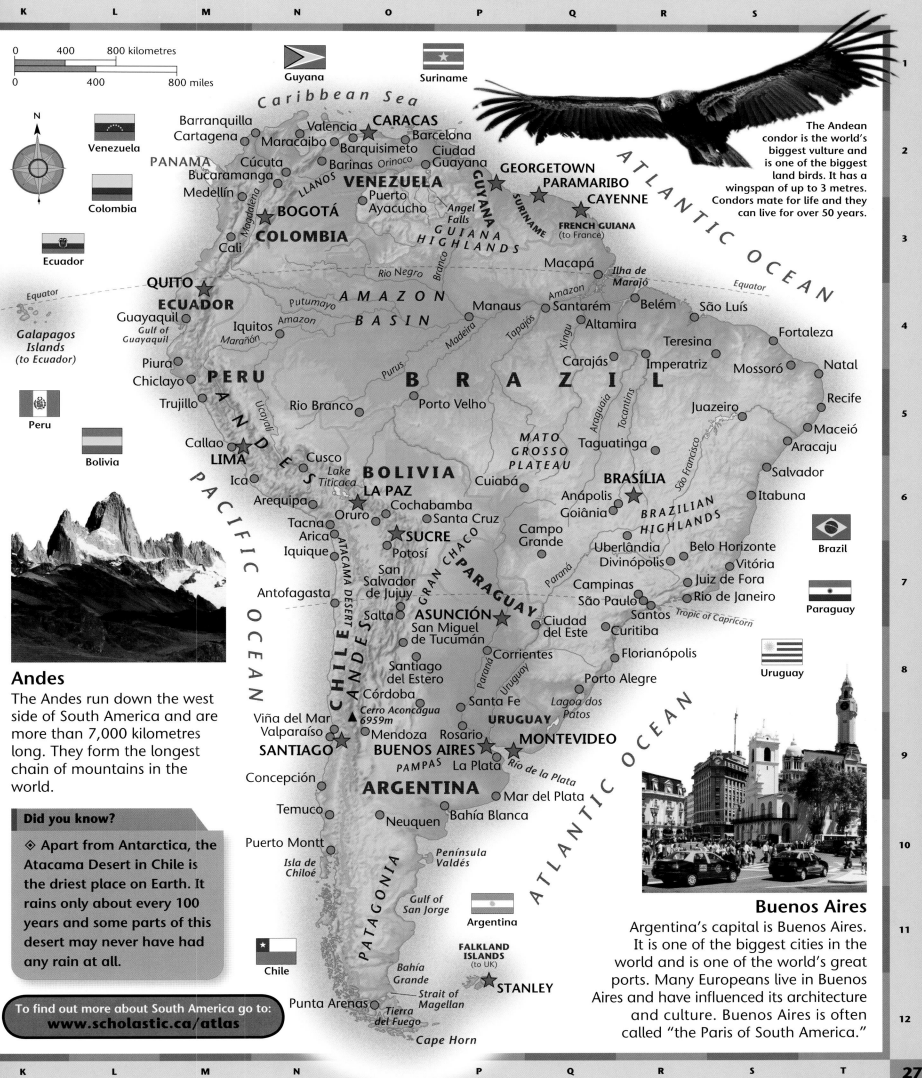

K L M N O P Q R S

0 400 800 kilometres
0 400 800 miles

N

Guyana

Suriname

Venezuela

Colombia

Ecuador

Peru

Bolivia

The Andean condor is the world's biggest vulture and is one of the biggest land birds. It has a wingspan of up to 3 metres. Condors mate for life and they can live for over 50 years.

Caribbean Sea

Barranquilla
Cartagena
Maracaibo
Valencia
CARACAS
Barcelona
Cúcuta
Barquisimeto
Ciudad
Guayana
PANAMA
Bucaramanga
Barinas
Orinoco
GEORGETOWN
PARAMARIBO
Medellín
LLANOS
VENEZUELA
GUYANA
SURINAME
CAYENNE
Magdalena
Puerto
Ayacucho
FRENCH GUIANA
(to France)
BOGOTÁ
Angel
Falls
COLOMBIA
GUIANA
HIGHLANDS
Cali
Macapá
Ilha de
Marajó
ATLANTIC OCEAN
Rio Negro
Branco
Equator

Equator
QUITO
ECUADOR
AMAZON
Amazon
Manaus
Santarém
Belém
São Luís
Galapagos
Islands
(to Ecuador)
Guayaquil
Putumayo
BASIN
Iquitos
Amazon
Altamira
Fortaleza
Gulf of
Guayaquil
Marañón
Madeira
Tapajós
Xingu
Teresina
Piura
Purus
Carajás
Imperatriz
Mossoró
Natal
Chiclayo
PERU
B R A Z I L
Trujillo
Uçayali
Rio Branco
Porto Velho
Juazeiro
Recife
A
N
Araguaia
Tocantins
Maceió
Callao
Cusco
MATO
Taguatinga
Aracaju
LIMA
D
Lake
GROSSO
São Francisco
Ica
E
Titicaca
PLATEAU
Salvador
Arequipa
S
BOLIVIA
Cuiabá
BRASÍLIA
Itabuna
PACIFIC OCEAN
LA PAZ
Anápolis
Oruro
Cochabamba
Goiânia
BRAZILIAN
Tacna
Santa Cruz
HIGHLANDS
Arica
SUCRE
Campo
Uberlândia
Belo Horizonte
Iquique
Potosí
Grande
Divinópolis
Vitória
San
GRAN CHACO
Paraná
Juiz de Fora
Brazil
Antofagasta
Salvador
de Jujuy
PARAGUAY
Campinas
Rio de Janeiro
ATACAMA DESERT
Salta
ASUNCIÓN
São Paulo
Santos
San Miguel
Ciudad
Tropic of Capricorn
Paraguay
de Tucumán
del Este
Curitiba
Corrientes
Florianópolis
Santiago
Paraná
del Estero
Uruguay
Porto Alegre
Uruguay
Córdoba
Santa Fe
Lagoa dos
Cerro Aconcagua
Patos
6959m
URUGUAY
Viña del Mar
Mendoza
Rosario
MONTEVIDEO
Valparaíso
SANTIAGO
BUENOS AIRES
PAMPAS
La Plata
Río de la Plata
Concepción
ARGENTINA
Mar del Plata
ATLANTIC OCEAN
Temuco
Bahía Blanca
Neuquen
Puerto Montt
Península
Valdés
Isla de
Chiloé
Argentina
PATAGONIA
Gulf of
San Jorge
FALKLAND
ISLANDS
(to UK)
Chile
Bahía
Grande
STANLEY
Punta Arenas
Tierra
del Fuego
Strait of
Magellan
Cape Horn

Andes

The Andes run down the west side of South America and are more than 7,000 kilometres long. They form the longest chain of mountains in the world.

Did you know?

◈ Apart from Antarctica, the Atacama Desert in Chile is the driest place on Earth. It rains only about every 100 years and some parts of this desert may never have had any rain at all.

To find out more about South America go to: www.scholastic.ca/atlas

Buenos Aires

Argentina's capital is Buenos Aires. It is one of the biggest cities in the world and is one of the world's great ports. Many Europeans live in Buenos Aires and have influenced its architecture and culture. Buenos Aires is often called "the Paris of South America."

Northern Africa
AFRICA

The continent of Africa is the second-largest in the world. Northern Africa is mostly covered by the Sahara, which is the world's largest hot desert. Few people live there because conditions are so harsh. Most people in Northern Africa live near the coast or along the River Nile. Crops such as dates, cork, grapes and olives are produced in the north of the region, and cocoa beans, peanuts and palm oil in the south. Textiles are made in every area, especially in the north, where rugs are produced. There are big deposits of oil and natural gas in Libya, and in countries such as Egypt, Tunisia and Morocco, tourism is important.

Country File

Algeria

Benin

Burkina Faso

Cameroon

Cape Verde

Central African Republic

Chad

Djibouti

Egypt

Eritrea

Ethiopia

Gambia

Ghana

Guinea

Guinea-Bissau

Ivory Coast

Liberia

Libya

Mali

Mauritania

Morocco

Niger

Nigeria

Senegal

Sierra Leone

Somalia

Sudan

Togo

Tunisia

Western Sahara

Did you know?
◈ Uranium, diamonds and gold are mined in northern Africa.

Did you know?
◈ Half of the world's cocoa beans are now grown in Northern Africa.

Tunisia

Algeria

Morocco

Western Sahara

Mauritania

Mali

Cape Verde

Senegal

Gambia

Guinea-Bissau

Guinea

Sierra Leone

Liberia

Ivory Coast

Burkina Faso

Ghana

Togo   Benin

Nigeria

M e d i t e r r

ALGIERS   TUNIS

Tanger   Oran   Constantine

RABAT   Sfax

Casablanca   TUNISIA

MOROCCO   ATLAS MOUNTAINS

Marrakech

ALGERIA

LAAYOUNE

WESTERN SAHARA   Tropic of Cancer   AHAGGAR

A T L A N T I C   O C E A N

S A H A R A

MAURITANIA

NOUAKCHOTT

MALI   NIGER

Agadez

Senegal

CAPE VERDE   S A H E L

PRAIA   SENEGAL   Niger

DAKAR   NIAMEY

GAMBIA   BAMAKO

BANJUL   OUAGADOUGOU

BISSAU   BURKINA FASO   NIGERIA

GUINEA-BISSAU   GUINEA

CONAKRY   IVORY COAST   ABUJA

FREETOWN   YAMOUSSOUKRO   PORTO-NOVO

SIERRA LEONE   Lagos

MONROVIA   LOME

LIBERIA   Abidjan   ACCRA   Gulf of   Douala

Guinea   YAOUNDE

EQUATORIAL GUINEA

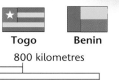

Fennec fox
This desert mammal's sandy colour helps it to hide from prey. It keeps cool by losing body heat through its huge ears. This fox usually hunts at night when it is cooler.

0   400   800 kilometres

0   400   800 miles

12

Did you know?

◈ Cairo, Egypt, is the largest city in Africa. Almost 16 million people live in this ancient city and its suburbs.

Peanuts are grown along the southern coast of northern Africa. Most of these nuts are made into cooking oil.

Sahara

Strong winds in the Sahara blow the sand into dunes over 430 metres high. This desert is getting bigger because the winds blow the sand and because people have cut down trees around the edges for fuel and to grow crops. In the south, people are planting grasses to try to stop the desert from spreading any further.

Did you know?

◈ "Sahara" is Arabic for desert. Less than 25 mm of rain falls there in a year.

Did you know?

◈ More dates are grown in Egypt than anywhere else in the world.

Scorpion

These creatures are found throughout northern Africa. Their hard, flat bodies protect them from the extremes of temperature and allow them to creep under rocks to hide from predators and the hot desert sun.

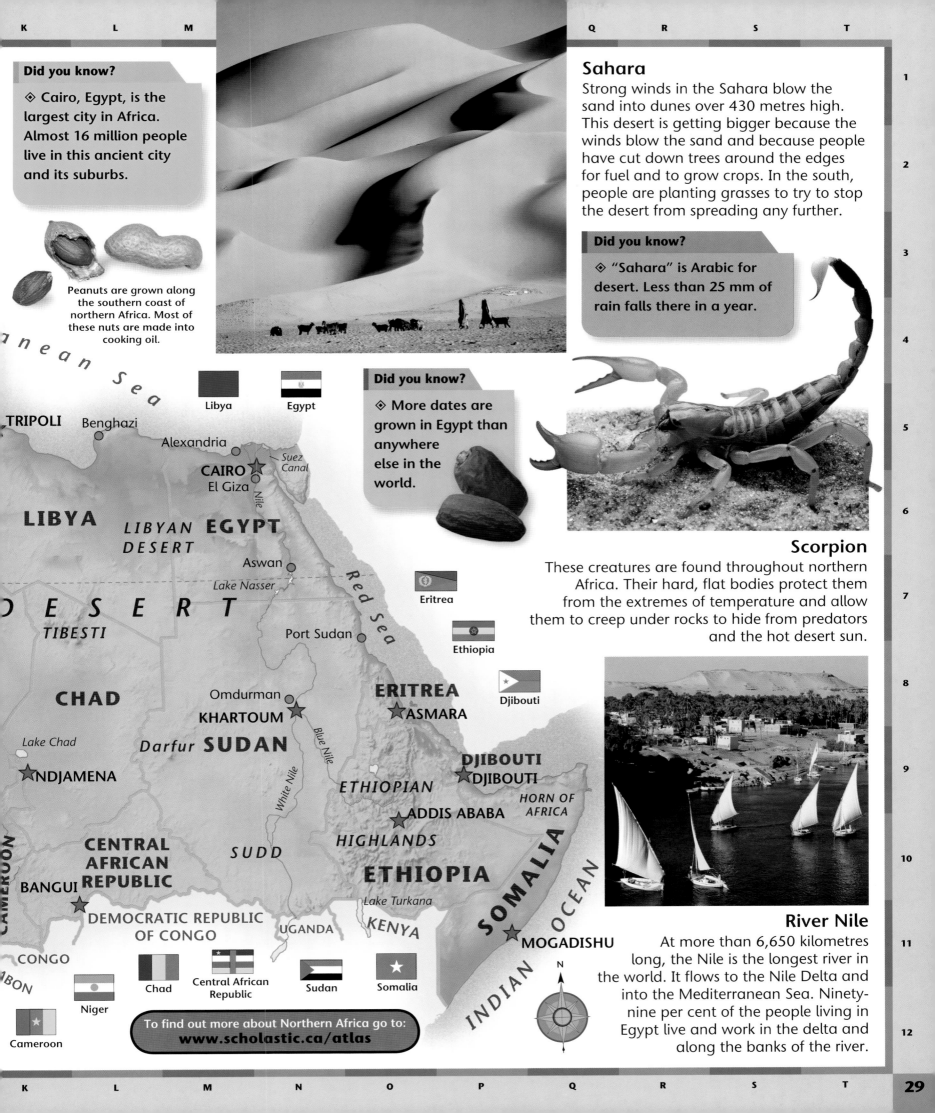

Libya

Egypt

Eritrea

Ethiopia

Djibouti

Chad

Central African Republic

Sudan

Somalia

Niger

Cameroon

TRIPOLI
Benghazi
Alexandria
Suez Canal
CAIRO
El Giza
Nile

LIBYA
LIBYAN DESERT
EGYPT

Aswan
Lake Nasser

D E S E R T
TIBESTI

Red Sea

Port Sudan

CHAD

Omdurman
KHARTOUM

Lake Chad
Darfur **SUDAN**

NDJAMENA

Blue Nile
White Nile

ERITREA
ASMARA

DJIBOUTI
DJIBOUTI

ETHIOPIAN

CENTRAL AFRICAN REPUBLIC

SUDD

ADDIS ABABA

HIGHLANDS

HORN OF AFRICA

ETHIOPIA

BANGUI

DEMOCRATIC REPUBLIC OF CONGO

Lake Turkana

UGANDA
KENYA

SOMALIA

MOGADISHU

CONGO

GABON

INDIAN OCEAN

N

River Nile

At more than 6,650 kilometres long, the Nile is the longest river in the world. It flows to the Nile Delta and into the Mediterranean Sea. Ninety-nine per cent of the people living in Egypt live and work in the delta and along the banks of the river.

To find out more about Northern Africa go to:
www.scholastic.ca/atlas

nean Sea

Southern Africa

AFRICA

Southern Africa has many different climates. The Congo Basin is hot and humid and is the site of the world's second biggest tropical rainforest. Further east and south are dry woodlands merging into savannah, which is a mixture of grassland and open woodland. It is there that the most well-known African animals are found. Farther south is the Namib Desert, one of the hottest and driest places on Earth, with temperatures over 50°C during the day. Hundreds of different tribes live in southern Africa. There are hundreds of languages. The Kalahari Desert in Botswana is home to one of the few remaining groups of hunter-gatherers, the Bushmen, or San. In the 19th century, large gold and diamond deposits were found in South Africa, helping it to become the most powerful country in Southern Africa.

Country File

- Angola
- Botswana
- Burundi
- Comoros
- Congo
- Democratic Republic of Congo
- Equatorial Guinea
- Gabon
- Kenya
- Lesotho
- Madagascar
- Malawi
- Mauritius
- Mozambique
- Namibia
- Rwanda
- Sao Tome and Principe
- Seychelles
- South Africa
- Swaziland
- Tanzania
- Uganda
- Zambia
- Zimbabwe

Many different crops are grown in Southern Africa, including citrus fruits and grapes, mainly for export.

Equatorial Guinea

Congo

Sao Tome and Principe

Gabon

Angola

Namibia

Botswana

South Africa

Victoria Falls

This famous waterfall is on the Zambezi River, on the border between Zambia and Zimbabwe. It is 108 metres high and 1,700 metres wide. Local people call it "the smoke that thunders" because of the loud noise and spray that it makes.

Did you know?

◈ Diamonds are the world's hardest natural substance. Half of all the world's diamonds are mined in Southern Africa.

African wildlife

Elephants, rhinoceroses, lions, leopards and buffalo are known as "the big five," and they attract thousands of tourists to Africa. Many are endangered species and they are protected by law.

South Africa

MALABO
EQUATORIAL GUINEA
SAO TOME
SAO TOME & PRINCIPE
BRAZZAVILLE
ANGOLA
LUANDA
CAMEROON
CENTRAL AFRIC
Ubang
Cong
LIBREVILLE
GABON
Mbandaka
CON
BAS.
CONGO
DEM
REP
O
KINSHASA
Kanang
ANGOLA
Huambo
BIÉ PLATEAU
Namibe
Lubango
NAMIBIA
WINDHOEK
KALAHA
DESERT
Orange River
SOUT
CAPE TOWN
Cape of Good Hope
ATLANTIC OCEAN
NAMIB DESERT

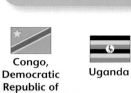

Congo, Democratic Republic of

Uganda

Kenya

Gorillas are the largest primates in the world (humans are primates too). These apes live in forests, in groups led by a large male.

Kilimanjaro

The top of Kilimanjaro in Tanzania is covered in snow all year round, even though the mountain is close to the Equator. This is because the temperature drops as the land gets higher. Kilimanjaro is 5,895 metres high. It is the highest point in Africa.

Rwanda

Burundi

Tanzania

Seychelles

SUDAN
ETHIOPIA
Lake Turkana
...PUBLIC
UGANDA
KAMPALA
KENYA
Kisangani
Kisumu Equator
SOMALIA
Lake Victoria
...RATIC
KIGALI RWANDA
NAIROBI
...LIC
BUJUMBURA BURUNDI
▲ Kilimanjaro 5895m
Mombasa
...ONGO
Lake Tanganyika
Olduvai Gorge
...buji-Mayi
DODOMA
Zanzibar
SEYCHELLES
TANZANIA
Dar es Salaam
Kolwezi
Lubumbashi
MALAWI
COMOROS
Comoros
Kitwe
Lake Nyasa
MORONI
Malawi
Ndola
LILONGWE
ZAMBIA
MAYOTTE (to France)
...USAKA
Zambezi
Blantyre
Zambia
Victoria Falls
Mauritius
HARARE
ANTANANARIVO
ZIMBABWE
MAURITIUS
Bulawayo
Beira
PORT LOUIS
...TSWANA
Limpopo
RÉUNION (to France)
...ABORONE
MADAGASCAR
TSHWANE (PRETORIA)
MBABANE
Tropic of Capricorn
MAPUTO
...weto
SWAZILAND
Johannesburg
Madagascar
...OEMFONTEIN
MASERU
...SOTHO
Durban
...RICA
DRAKENSBERG
Zimbabwe
INDIAN OCEAN
Mozambique
Port Elizabeth
Swaziland
Mozambique Channel
MOZAMBIQUE

N

Baobab tree

The island of Madagascar, off the eastern coast of Africa, split off from the mainland millions of years ago. Many unique and unusual species of plants and animals developed there. Several types of baobab tree grow only in Madagascar. Some of these extraordinary trees are over 3,000 years old.

South Africa's climate is varied and is suitable for growing many types of cut flower, such as gerberas, roses and carnations. These are all exported to Europe, as well as being sold locally.

To find out more about Southern Africa go to:
www.scholastic.ca/atlas

Lesotho

0 400 800 kilometres

0 400 800 miles

Northern Europe

EUROPE

Norway, Sweden and Denmark are known as Scandinavia. The countries of Estonia, Latvia and Lithuania are called the Baltic States. These six countries, together with Finland and Iceland, are the most northern in Europe. Most people in Scandinavia live in the cities or towns in the south and around the coast. Throughout Scandinavia there are forests, and many of the trees are used to make furniture and paper. Iron ore is used for making steel, and the water from the lakes and rivers is used to produce hydroelectricity. There are plenty of fish in the coastal waters of northern Europe, and all these countries have strong fishing industries.

Country File

Denmark

Estonia

Finland

Iceland

Latvia

Lithuania

Norway

Sweden

Lapland

The northern part of Norway, Sweden and Finland is known as Lapland. This is the home of the Sami people. Some Sami still herd reindeer, which they keep for their milk, meat and skins.

Norwegian fjords

Fjords are long, deep, steep-sided valleys, which glaciers carved through the mountains over 150,000 years ago. As the ice melted, the sea levels rose and the valleys flooded with water. Thousands of tourists visit the fjords each year to enjoy the beautiful scenery.

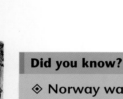

Red squirrel

The red squirrel lives all over northern Europe. Although it is called "red" it can be black, brown or red with a pale belly. Other mammals, such as brown bears, elk and grey wolves, are also found in the forests of Scandinavia.

Did you know?

◈ Norway was rated the world's most peaceful country on the 2007 Global Peace Index.

Two-thirds of the land in Denmark is used for farming. Most of it is used for pig farming or for growing food for the pigs.

Did you know?

◈ Finland has more than 188,000 lakes, and three-quarters of the country is covered by forest.

◈ Denmark has some of the longest beaches in Europe.

Timber for building

Wood is a very important material for all of the countries in northern Europe. Over the centuries wood has been used for producing fuel, for making furniture and toys, and for building houses and churches. There are so many trees in this area that many houses and public buildings are still made from wood today.

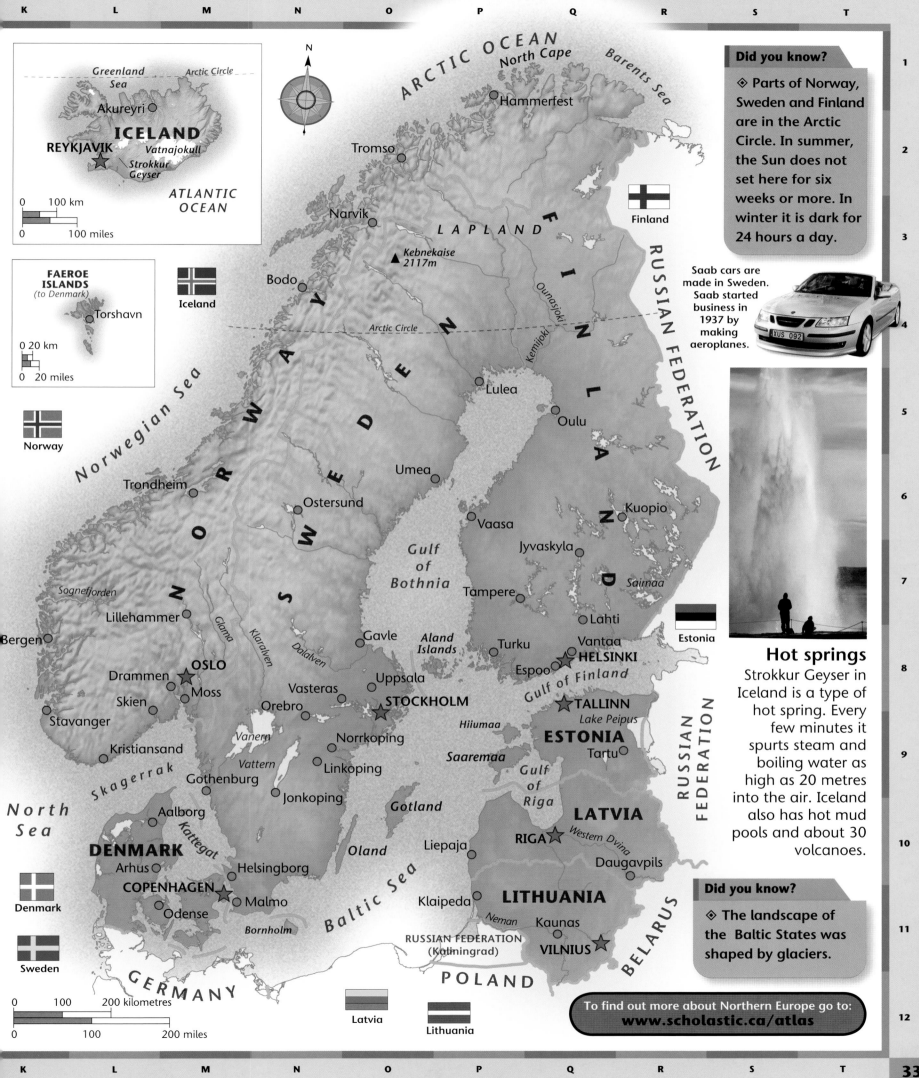

ICELAND

Akureyri

REYKJAVIK

Vatnajokull

Strokkur Geyser

ATLANTIC OCEAN

Greenland Sea   *Arctic Circle*

0   100 km
0   100 miles

FAEROE ISLANDS
(to Denmark)

Torshavn

0 20 km
0 20 miles

Norway

Iceland

Finland

Norwegian Sea

ARCTIC OCEAN

North Cape

Barents Sea

Hammerfest

Tromso

Narvik

LAPLAND

Bodo

▲ Kebnekaise 2117m

Ounasjoki

RUSSIAN FEDERATION

Kemijoki

Arctic Circle

F I N L A N D

N O R W A Y

S W E D E N

Sognefjorden

Trondheim

Ostersund

Lulea

Oulu

Umea

Kuopio

Vaasa

Jyvaskyla

Saimaa

Lillehammer

Tampere

Lahti

Glama

Klaralven

Dalalven

Gavle

Aland Islands

Turku

Vantaa

Espoo HELSINKI

Gulf of Finland

Bergen

Gulf of Bothnia

Stavanger

Skien

Moss

Drammen OSLO

Vasteras

Uppsala

STOCKHOLM

TALLINN

Lake Peipus

Hiiumaa

ESTONIA

Tartu

Estonia

Kristiansand

Vanern

Orebro

Norrkoping

Saaremaa

Vattern

Linkoping

Gulf of Riga

Gothenburg

Jonkoping

Gotland

LATVIA

North Sea

Skagerrak

Oland

Liepaja

RIGA

Western Dvina

DENMARK

Aalborg

Kattegat

Daugavpils

Arhus

Helsingborg

Klaipeda

LITHUANIA

COPENHAGEN

Malmo

Baltic Sea

Kaunas

Odense

Neman

Bornholm

RUSSIAN FEDERATION
(Kaliningrad)

VILNIUS

BELARUS

Denmark

Sweden

Latvia

Lithuania

GERMANY

POLAND

0   100   200 kilometres
0   100   200 miles

To find out more about Northern Europe go to:
www.scholastic.ca/atlas

Did you know?

◈ Parts of Norway, Sweden and Finland are in the Arctic Circle. In summer, the Sun does not set here for six weeks or more. In winter it is dark for 24 hours a day.

Saab cars are made in Sweden. Saab started business in 1937 by making aeroplanes.

Hot springs

Strokkur Geyser in Iceland is a type of hot spring. Every few minutes it spurts steam and boiling water as high as 20 metres into the air. Iceland also has hot mud pools and about 30 volcanoes.

Did you know?

◈ The landscape of the Baltic States was shaped by glaciers.

Western Europe

EUROPE

The area in Europe that is furthest from Asia is known as western Europe. The most northern countries have a mild, wet climate. Further south the climate becomes increasingly warm. In southern France, Spain and Portugal, the temperature in summer often reaches over 30°C. The land is suitable for many kinds of farming. Oranges are grown in Spain, flowers in the Netherlands, and wheat and potatoes throughout western Europe. Many countries also grow grapes to make wine. Wine-making is important in France, Spain and Portugal. Most people in western Europe live in large towns and cities. Tourism is a big industry. Electronics and car manufacturing are also major industries in western Europe.

Country File

Andorra

Belgium

France

Ireland

Luxembourg

Monaco

Netherlands

Portugal

Spain

United Kingdom

Red fox

Foxes are members of the dog family. They are found all across Europe and survive in towns and cities as well as the countryside. They eat all kinds of things, such as worms, berries, insects, small mammals and household waste.

Did you know?

◇ Only 26 land mammal species are native to Ireland.

The fastest train in the world is the French TGV *Train à Grande Vitesse*, which travels at an average speed of 300 km per hour.

Did you know?

◇ People from South America, Indonesia and the Caribbean make up five per cent of the population of the Netherlands. There used to be Dutch colonies in these places.

Over 500 different varieties of cheese are made in France, including brie and roquefort.

Costa Brava

The coastal region in northeast Spain known as the Costa Brava stretches for about 160 kilometres along the Mediterranean Sea. It is popular for its sandy beaches and its warm seas. The area is also an important cork-growing region and supplies cork to wine producers all over the world.

London Eye

Millions of tourists visit London every year for its history, theatres and sights, such as Big Ben and the London Eye. The London Eye is the world's tallest observation wheel, at 135 metres high. About 3.5 million people visit it each year to see the view from the top. Passengers can see for 40 kilometres in all directions.

Did you know?

◇ The southern tip of Spain is only 13 km from Africa at its closest point.

◇ Belgium is famous for making chocolate and produces 172,000 tonnes of chocolates every year.

Grapes grow on plants called vines, and the areas where wine is produced are called vineyards.

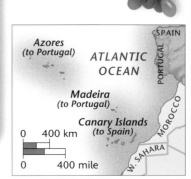

Azores (to Portugal)

ATLANTIC OCEAN

SPAIN

PORTUGAL

Madeira (to Portugal)

Canary Islands (to Spain)

MOROCCO

W. SAHARA

0   400 km

0   400 mile

6
7
8
9
10
11
12

Did you know?

❖ Half of the Netherlands is the same height or lower than the level of the sea. Flooding is a constant threat in this country.

Did you know?

❖ The United Kingdom and Ireland together are called the British Isles. They consist of over 6,000 small islands.

❖ The guitar is Spain's national instrument.

Map labels

Outer
Hebrides

Orkney
Islands

Inverness

Aberdeen

SCOTLAND

Dundee

Glasgow   Edinburgh

Ireland

NORTHERN
IRELAND
Belfast

Newcastle
upon Tyne

UNITED
KINGDOM

Galway   DUBLIN   Manchester   Leeds

IRELAND   Liverpool   Sheffield

Limerick   ENGLAND
             Birmingham

Cork   WALES

United Kingdom   Cardiff   LONDON

Bristol

Southampton

Plymouth   English Channel

CHANNEL ISLANDS   Le Havre
(to UK)

Brest

Luxembourg

France

Bay of
Biscay

North
Sea

Belgium   Netherlands

Groningen

NETHERLANDS
THE   AMSTERDAM
HAGUE   Utrecht

Rotterdam   Eindhoven

Antwerp

Ghent   BRUSSELS

Lille   BELGIUM

Amiens   LUXEMBOURG
Reims   LUXEMBOURG

Seine

PARIS   Strasbourg

Rennes   Orléans

Meuse

Dijon

Loire

Nantes

FRANCE

SWITZERLAND

Rhine

Mt Blanc
4807m

Limoges   Clermont-
             Ferrand   Lyon

ALPS

ITALY

Bordeaux   St-Étienne
             Grenoble

Dordogne

MASSIF
CENTRAL

Rhône

Garonne

A Coruña   Gijón   Santander

Oviedo   Bilbao

Vigo   Vitoria-Gasteiz

Ebro

Braga   Valladolid   Zaragoza

Viana do Castelo

Oporto   Duero

Spain   Coimbra

PORTUGAL

LISBON

Portugal   Setúbal

Tagus

Mérida   Guadiana

Seville   Córdoba

Faro

Málaga

Gibraltar (to UK)

AFRICA

Toulouse   Montpellier

ANDORRA

Perpignan

Costa Brava

Lleida

Barcelona

SPAIN

MADRID

Toledo

Valencia

Albacete

Majorca   Minorca

Palma

Ibiza   Balearic Islands

Alicante

Murcia

Granada

Andorra

Nice

MONACO

Marseille

Monaco

Corsica

Ajaccio

Mediterranean Sea

ATLANTIC OCEAN

N

Tulip fields

The Netherlands is famous for its flower bulbs. It produces 9 billion bulbs every year. In spring the Dutch tulip fields near Amsterdam are ablaze with colour. Visitors come from all over the world to see them.

Hedgehog

This small mammal lives in many parts of Europe. It has thousands of short spines over its back. If danger threatens, it rolls itself into a prickly ball.

Eiffel Tower

This famous European landmark is in Paris, France. The Eiffel Tower is 324 metres high, including the TV antenna on top. It is made almost entirely of wrought iron.

0   100   200 kilometres

0   100   200 miles

To find out more about Western Europe go to:
www.scholastic.ca/atlas

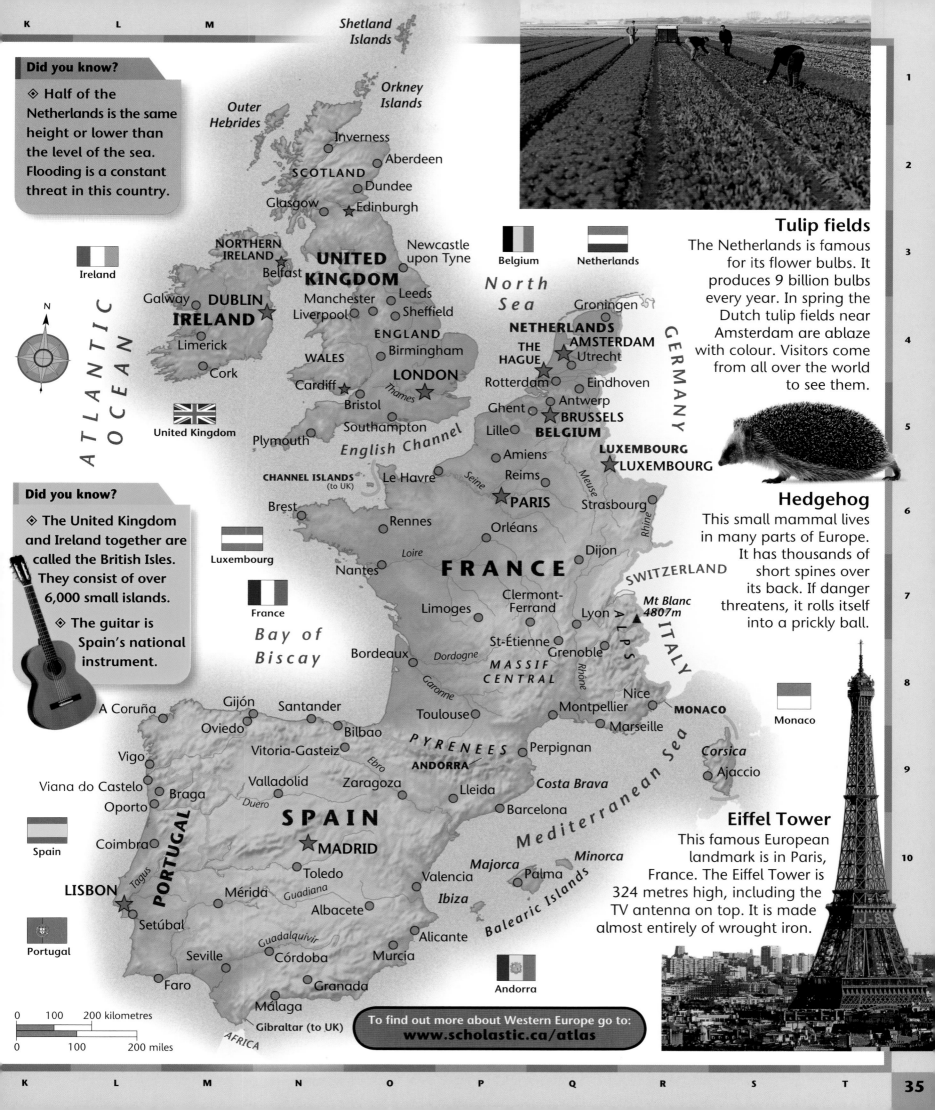

Central Europe

EUROPE

The central part of Europe stretches from the Baltic Sea in the north to the Mediterranean Sea in the south. Winters can be very cold in the north, but the weather gets warmer the farther south you go. In Germany and Poland, land is used for mining, industry and farming. People grow crops such as potatoes and barley, and many farmers keep pigs and goats. Farther south, especially in Italy, people grow olives, grapes and citrus fruit. Many long rivers run through central Europe, including the Rhine and the Danube. People use these rivers for transporting their goods. A high mountain range called the Alps runs through France, Switzerland, Austria and northern Italy.

Country File

Austria

Czech Republic

Germany

Italy

Liechtenstein

Malta

Poland

San Marino

Slovakia

Slovenia

Switzerland

Vatican City

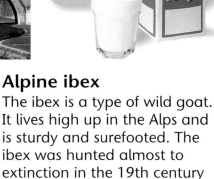

Alps

This range of mountains is mainly in France, Italy, Switzerland and Austria and is about 1,200 kilometres long. Many people visit the Alps to climb, walk and ski.

Did you know?

◈ Brown coal (lignite) is central Europe's main fuel and is one of Poland's main exports. It contains lots of sulphur, and burning it to make electricity adds to air pollution and acid rain.

Lamborghini cars are made in Italy. They are some of the fastest, most expensive sports cars in the world.

Did you know?

◈ Germany produces enough milk for its whole population.

Vatican City

The Vatican City is in Rome, Italy. It is the smallest country in the world and it takes up an area of only 440,000 square metres. It contains St Peter's Basilica and the Apostolic Palace, where the pope lives.

Tomatoes and basil are important ingredients in many Italian dishes.

Alpine ibex

The ibex is a type of wild goat. It lives high up in the Alps and is sturdy and surefooted. The ibex was hunted almost to extinction in the 19th century but now its numbers are growing.

National parks

There are many national parks in central Europe. This is Triglav National Park in Slovenia. It contains Triglav mountain, which is the highest peak in Slovenia. There are beech and spruce forests, and animals such as chamois and lynx live here.

Did you know?

◈ Pizza and pasta are traditional Italian foods, but they are now enjoyed all over the world.

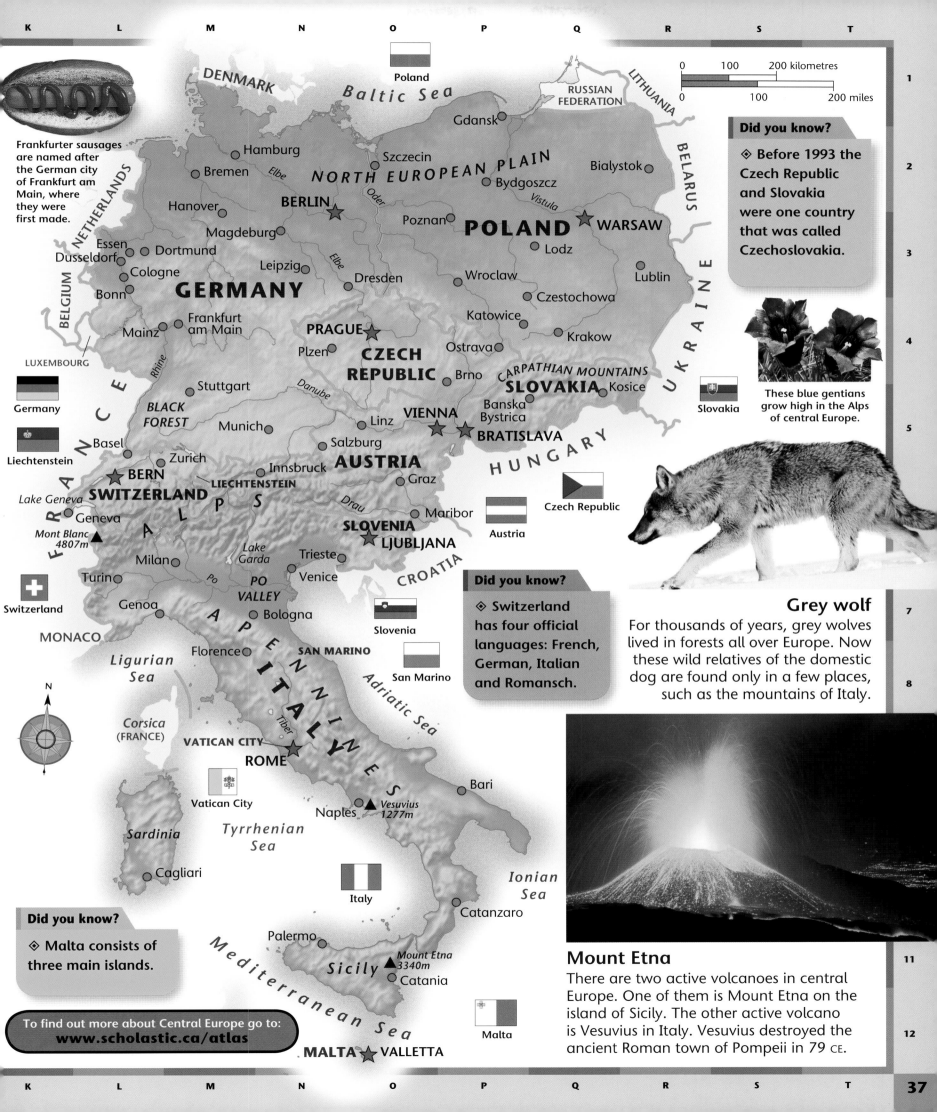

1

2

3

4

5

7

8

11

12

Frankfurter sausages are named after the German city of Frankfurt am Main, where they were first made.

Did you know?

◈ Before 1993 the Czech Republic and Slovakia were one country that was called Czechoslovakia.

These blue gentians grow high in the Alps of central Europe.

Grey wolf

For thousands of years, grey wolves lived in forests all over Europe. Now these wild relatives of the domestic dog are found only in a few places, such as the mountains of Italy.

Did you know?

◈ Switzerland has four official languages: French, German, Italian and Romansch.

Did you know?

◈ Malta consists of three main islands.

To find out more about Central Europe go to:
www.scholastic.ca/atlas

Mount Etna

There are two active volcanoes in central Europe. One of them is Mount Etna on the island of Sicily. The other active volcano is Vesuvius in Italy. Vesuvius destroyed the ancient Roman town of Pompeii in 79 CE.

0   100   200 kilometres
0   100   200 miles

Map labels:

DENMARK
Baltic Sea
RUSSIAN FEDERATION
LITHUANIA
BELARUS
Poland
Gdansk
NORTH EUROPEAN PLAIN
Hamburg
Bremen
Szczecin
Bialystok
Elbe
Bydgoszcz
Hanover
BERLIN
Oder
POLAND
WARSAW
Magdeburg
Poznan
Vistula
NETHERLANDS
Essen
Dortmund
Leipzig
Lodz
Dusseldorf
Cologne
Dresden
Wroclaw
Lublin
Bonn
GERMANY
Czestochowa
UKRAINE
BELGIUM
Mainz
Frankfurt am Main
Katowice
Krakow
LUXEMBOURG
Plzen
PRAGUE
CZECH REPUBLIC
Ostrava
Brno
CARPATHIAN MOUNTAINS
SLOVAKIA
Kosice
Germany
Stuttgart
Danube
Banska Bystrica
Slovakia
FRANCE
BLACK FOREST
Munich
Linz
VIENNA
BRATISLAVA
Liechtenstein
Basel
Salzburg
AUSTRIA
HUNGARY
Czech Republic
Zurich
Innsbruck
Graz
BERN
LIECHTENSTEIN
SWITZERLAND
Austria
Lake Geneva
ALPS
Drau
Maribor
Geneva
SLOVENIA
LJUBLJANA
Mont Blanc 4807m
Milan
Lake Garda
Trieste
Switzerland
Turin
Po
PO VALLEY
Venice
CROATIA
Slovenia
Genoa
Bologna
MONACO
Ligurian Sea
Florence
SAN MARINO
APENNINES
San Marino
Corsica (FRANCE)
ITALY
Adriatic Sea
Tiber
VATICAN CITY
ROME
Vatican City
Bari
Naples
Vesuvius 1277m
Italy
Sardinia
Tyrrhenian Sea
Cagliari
Ionian Sea
Catanzaro
Palermo
Mediterranean Sea
Sicily
Mount Etna 3340m
Catania
Malta
MALTA
VALLETTA

Southeast Europe
EUROPE

Much of this area is mountainous, although there are fertile, flat areas in the north and east. Farming is important in these countries and many crops, such as grapes, tobacco, roses and wheat, are grown. In the north, the winters are very cold. Further south and around the coast, winters are milder and summers are hot and dry. During the past 30 years there have been many changes and wars in southeast Europe, caused by political, ethnic and religious problems. In the 1990s, Ukraine, Belarus and Moldova gained independence from the former Soviet Union. The former Yugoslavia split into the republics of Croatia, Serbia, Bosnia and Herzegovina, Macedonia and Montenegro. After years of war, some areas are still recovering from their problems.

Country File

- Albania
- Belarus
- Bosnia and Herzegovina
- Bulgaria
- Croatia
- Greece
- Hungary
- Macedonia
- Moldova
- Montenegro
- Romania
- Serbia
- Ukraine

Most of the world's rose oil is produced in Bulgaria. Rose oil is used in luxury perfumes, soaps and cosmetics.

Did you know?

◈ Some of the water from the springs in Budapest is over 90°C. It has to be mixed with cold water before it can be used.

Dubrovnik

The town of Dubrovnik in Croatia is encircled by 1,940 metres of city walls, which were built over 400 years ago. There are several towers and fortresses along the walls, making it one of the strongest fortifications in Europe.

Did you know?

◈ The European bison has been reintroduced to the Byelavyezhskaya forest in Belarus and Poland. It was extinct in the wild.

Budapest

The Hungarian city of Budapest sits on a geological fault line. There are more than 120 springs in the city, where hot water rises naturally from the ground. People have built spas and baths over the hot springs for almost 2,000 years.

Wild boar

There are wild boars roaming freely throughout the forests of southeast Europe. These nocturnal animals forage for food from dusk until dawn. They live in groups called sounders, containing about 20 animals. The groups are made up of three or four females and their young.

Olives have been grown in Greece for over 2,000 years, and olives and olive oil are major exports. Olives are also important ingredients in many dishes.

Acropolis

Athens, the capital of Greece, is named after Athena, the goddess of war in Greek mythology. The Parthenon is Athena's chief temple. It was built in the 5th century BCE on the Acropolis hill above Athens. Acropolis means "edge of the city."

Ukraine

The rich, dark soil of Ukraine is ideal for farming. Formerly part of the Soviet Union, Ukraine used to be known as "the bread basket of Russia." Today it exports large amounts of grain, vegetables, dairy products, meat and sunflower seeds.

Did you know?

◈ One in four people in Ukraine works in agriculture (farming) or forestry.

Much of the soil in Moldova is rich and fertile. Many vegetables are grown there, but grapes and sunflowers are the most important crops.

Pine marten

These animals are related to weasels and are about the size of a domestic cat. They live in wooded areas all over Europe and spend a lot of their time in trees, where they build their dens. Pine martens feed mostly on small mammals, birds, frogs, insects and carrion.

Did you know?

◈ The spotted Dalmatian dog gets its name from the Dalmatia region of Croatia.

To find out more about Southeast Europe go to:
www.scholastic.ca/atlas

Map labels

Belarus
Ukraine

LITHUANIA
LATVIA
Vitsyebsk
BELARUS
MINSK
Mahilyow
Hrodna
RUSSIAN FEDERATION
Babruysk
Homyel'
Dnieper
Brest
Pripet
Pripet Marshes
Chernihiv
POLAND
Chernobyl'
Luts'k
KIEV
Zhytomyr
Kharkiv
Donets
UKRAINE
Poltava
Luhans'k
L'viv
Cherkasy
Dnipropetrovs'k
Ivano-Frankivs'k
Kirovohrad
Dnieper
Donets'k
Chernivtsi
Dniester
Zaporizhzhya
CARPATHIAN MOUNTAINS
MOLDOVA
Southern Bug
Kryvyy Rih
Mariupol'
Iasi
CHISINAU
Mykolayiv
Bosnia and Herzegovina
Hungary
SLOVAKIA
Miskolc
Nyiregyhaza
Prut
Bacau
BLACK SEA LOWLAND
Sea of Azov
AUSTRIA
Gyor
Tisza
Cluj-Napoca
Tiraspol'
Croatia
BUDAPEST
Debrecen
Transylvania
Odesa
SLOVENIA
HUNGARY
Szeged
ROMANIA
Crimea
Drava
Pecs
Simferopol'
Moldova
ZAGREB
Timisoara
TRANSYLVANIAN ALPS
Brasov
Rijeka
CROATIA
Osijek
Novi Sad
Galati
Black Sea
Banja Luka
Sava
Ploiesti
Braila
Zadar
Tuzla
BUCHAREST
BOSNIA & HERZEGOVINA
BELGRADE
Craiova
Constanta
Serbia
SARAJEVO
SERBIA
Danube
Ruse
Romania
Split
Mostar
Nis
Montana
Dubrovnik
BULGARIA
Varna
Montenegro
MONTENEGRO
Pristina
BALKAN MOUNTAINS
PODGORICA
RHODOPE
SOFIA
Sliven
Burgas
Shkoder
Musala 2925m
Plovdiv
Bulgaria
SKOPJE
MOUNTAINS
Durres
MACEDONIA
Komotini
Albania
TIRANA
Bitola
Kavala
Lake Ohrid
Lake Prespa
Salonica
Macedonia
ALBANIA
TURKEY
Kerkyra
PINDOS MOUNTAINS
Larisa
Aegean Sea
Corfu
Arta
GREECE
Lesbos Sea
Lamia
Greece
Ionian Sea
Patra
ATHENS
Piraeus
TURKEY
Peloponnese
Dodecanese
Cyclades
Rhodes
Sea of Crete
Mediterranean Sea
Irakleio
Crete

0 100 200 kilometres
0 100 200 miles

Russian Federation

EUROPE AND ASIA

The Russian Federation is the largest country in the world. It stretches across two continents. The area to the west of the Ural Mountains is in Europe, and the area to the east is in Asia. Russia's climate varies massively, from Arctic weather in the north to mild weather in the south. More than three-quarters of the country is occupied by Siberia, but less than 30 per cent of the population lives there because the region has such long, cold winters. Siberia contains huge deposits of oil and natural gas. Russia also has fertile farmland and rich mineral deposits. Its main exports are oil and oil products, natural gas, metals, wood and wood products. Most of the people there are Russians, but there are more than 120 other ethnic groups with many different religions, languages and cultures.

Country File

Russian Federation

Russian Federation

Franz Josef Land

NORWAY
Murmansk
KOLA PENINSULA
FINLAND
Arctic Circle
Barents Sea
Novaya Zemlya
Kara Sea
White Sea
KALININGRAD (to Russia)
Kaliningrad
ESTONIA
Lake Ladoga
POLAND
LITH.
LATVIA
Petrozavodsk
St Petersburg
Lake Onega
Archangel
Pechora
Vorkuta
YAMAL PENINSULA
Velikiy Novgorod
BELARUS
Northern Dvina
NORTH EUROPEAN PLAIN
Tver'
Syktyvkar
Ob'
MOSCOW
Yaroslavl'
Tula
Ryazan'
Nizhniy Novgorod
Kirov
URAL MOUNTAINS
WEST SIBERIAN PLAIN
UKRAINE
Don
CENTRAL RUSSIAN UPLAND
Voronezh
Kazan'
Izhevsk
Perm'
R U S
Penza
Ul'yanovsk
Ob'
Rostov-na-Donu
Saratov
Volga
Yekaterinburg
Samara
Ufa
Tyumen
S
Volgograd
Trans-Siberian Railway
Krasnodar
Orenburg
Chelyabinsk
Irtysh
Stavropol'
Omsk
Tomsk
El'brus 5642m
Astrakhan'
Novosibirsk
CAUCASUS
Ob'
Kemerov
GEORGIA
Groznyy
Caspian Sea
K A Z A K H S T A N
Barnaul
AZERBAIJAN
Novokuznetsk

St Basil's Cathedral

St Basil's in Moscow is one of the most famous buildings in the world. It was built in Red Square by Tsar Ivan IV and was finished in 1560, after five years of building. It is actually eight separate churches, joined together with a central tower.

Did you know?

◈ Russia has two great classical ballet companies, called the Bolshoi and Mariinsky (formerly called the Kirov), which are both famous around the world.

Siberian tiger

The Siberian tiger is in danger of extinction. Its habitat is being destroyed and it is hunted for its body parts, which are used in traditional Chinese medicine. There are only about 500 left in the wild.

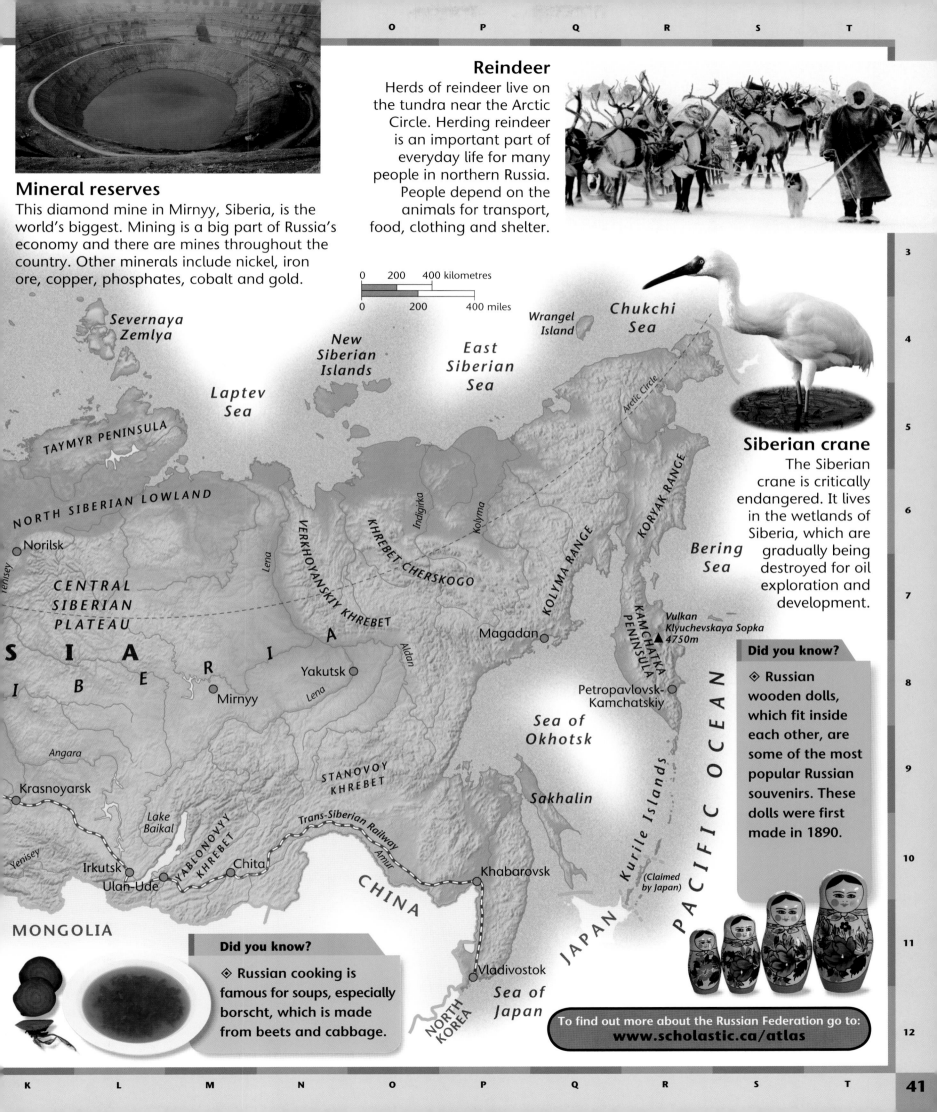

Mineral reserves

This diamond mine in Mirnyy, Siberia, is the world's biggest. Mining is a big part of Russia's economy and there are mines throughout the country. Other minerals include nickel, iron ore, copper, phosphates, cobalt and gold.

Reindeer

Herds of reindeer live on the tundra near the Arctic Circle. Herding reindeer is an important part of everyday life for many people in northern Russia. People depend on the animals for transport, food, clothing and shelter.

Siberian crane

The Siberian crane is critically endangered. It lives in the wetlands of Siberia, which are gradually being destroyed for oil exploration and development.

Did you know?

◈ Russian wooden dolls, which fit inside each other, are some of the most popular Russian souvenirs. These dolls were first made in 1890.

Did you know?

◈ Russian cooking is famous for soups, especially borscht, which is made from beets and cabbage.

To find out more about the Russian Federation go to:
www.scholastic.ca/atlas

0   200   400 kilometres
0   200   400 miles

Severnaya Zemlya

New Siberian Islands

Wrangel Island

Chukchi Sea

East Siberian Sea

Laptev Sea

TAYMYR PENINSULA

NORTH SIBERIAN LOWLAND

Yenisey

Norilsk

Lena

VERKHOYANSKIY KHREBET

Indigirka

KHREBET CHERSKOGO

Kolyma

KOLYMA RANGE

KORYAK RANGE

Arctic Circle

Bering Sea

CENTRAL SIBERIAN PLATEAU

S I B E R I A

Aldan

Magadan

KAMCHATKA PENINSULA

Vulkan Klyuchevskaya Sopka 4750m

Yakutsk

Mirnyy

Lena

Petropavlovsk-Kamchatskiy

Sea of Okhotsk

Angara

STANOVOY KHREBET

Sakhalin

Krasnoyarsk

Lake Baikal

YABLONOVYY KHREBET

Trans-Siberian Railway

Amur

Kurile Islands

PACIFIC OCEAN

Yenisey

Irkutsk

Ulan-Ude

Chita

Khabarovsk

CHINA

(Claimed by Japan)

MONGOLIA

Vladivostok

Sea of Japan

JAPAN

NORTH KOREA

Southwest Asia

ASIA

Almost all of Southwest Asia is desert. Temperatures can soar to over 30°C in the summer and very little rain falls. Although the weather is hot and dry, people have lived here, in cities and towns, for over 7,000 years. Three of the world's most important religions started here: Christianity, Islam and Judaism. This area has suffered wars for thousands of years and the conflicts still continue. The biggest source of income for many of these countries is from oil and gas. Tourism is an important industry in several countries, including Turkey and Israel. Turkey and Iran are famous for carpets, which are exported around the world.

Country File

Armenia

Azerbaijan

Bahrain

Cyprus

Georgia

Iran

Iraq

Israel

Jordan

Kuwait

Lebanon

Oman

Qatar

Saudi Arabia

Syria

Turkey

United Arab Emirates

Yemen

Cyprus · BULGARIA · Istanbul · Bursa · GREECE · Izmir · Denizli · TURKISH REPUBLIC O NORTHERN CYPRU (recognized only by Turkey)

Syria

Med

Lebanon

Mecca

The Ka'bah, a shrine inside the Sacred Mosque in Mecca in Saudi Arabia, is regarded by Muslims as the most sacred place on Earth.

Eggplants, apricots, pistachios and walnuts are important crops in this area.

Petra

The ancient city of Petra, in Jordan, lies deep inside a desert gorge. Most of the buildings were carved out of solid rock. Once, this ruined city was the capital of an Arab kingdom. Now it is a popular tourist attraction.

Did you know?

◈ Turkey is one of the few countries in the world that produces enough food for all its people. Half of the land in Turkey is used for agriculture (farming).

Dubai

The Burj al-Arab hotel in Dubai, in the United Arab Emirates, was the tallest hotel in the world when it opened in 1999. It is 321 metres high and has a helicopter pad on the 28th floor. The hotel stands on an artificial island, and was designed to look like a big sail.

Arabian oryx

The Arabian oryx was hunted to extinction in the wild. Then, after a worldwide breeding program in zoos, it was re-introduced into the wild in Oman. Today there are two herds of oryx roaming freely.

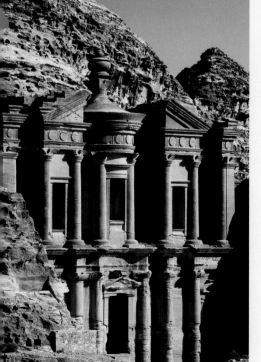

Turkey

Georgia

RUSSIAN
FEDERATION

Armenia

Azerbaijan

Dead Sea

The Dead Sea lies between Israel and Jordan.
It is almost nine times saltier than normal
sea water and no animals can live in it. It is
impossible to sink in the salty water.

Black Sea

C A U C A S U S

Kazbek 5047m ▲

K'ut'aisi

GEORGIA
T'BILISI ⭐

Iraq

Samsun

Trabzon

Erzurum

ARMENIA

AZERBAIJAN

BAKU ⭐

-skisehir

Kizil Irmak

⭐**ANKARA**

T U R K E Y

Euphrates

Mt. Ararat
5137m ▲

⭐**YEREVAN**

Aras

Kura

*Caspian
Sea*

T U R K M E N I S T A N

Iran

*Lake
Tuz*

Kayseri

Malatya

AZERBAIJAN

-onya

TAURUS MOUNTAINS

Adana

Diyarbakir

Van

*Lake
Van*

Tabriz

Rasht

Mashhad

ntalya

Gaziantep

Orumiyeh

*Lake
Urmia*

TEHRAN ⭐

▲ *Mount
Damavand
5671m*

A F G H A N I S T A N

Iran

Mersin

Aleppo

Mosul

Irbil

Hamadan

Qom

DASHT-E KAVIR

Kuwait

NICOSIA ⭐

Homs

SYRIA

Kirkuk

Kermanshah

Arak

I R A N

CYPRUS

LEBANON

BEIRUT ⭐

Tigris

IRAQ

Esfahan

Yazd

*IRANIAN
PLATEAU*

Kerman

DASHT-E LUT

Bahrain

-ranean
Sea

⭐**DAMASCUS**

*SYRIAN
DESERT*

Euphrates

BAGHDAD ⭐

Karbala

An Najaf

Al Kut

Ahvaz

Shiraz

Zahedan

Qatar

JERUSALEM

WEST BANK

⭐**AMMAN**

An Nasiriyah

Basra

P A K I S T A N

GAZA STRIP

ISRAEL

*Dead
Sea*

◇ Petra

JORDAN

KUWAIT
⭐**KUWAIT**

Bandar-e Bushehr

EGYPT

Tabuk

*AN
NAFUD*

The Gulf

Bandar-e
'Abbas

Israel

AD DAHNA

Ad Damman

Buraydah

Al Hufuf

BAHRAIN
MANAMA
QATAR
⭐**DOHA**

Strait of Hormuz

Dubai

OMAN

Gulf of Oman

N

*R
e
d

S
e
a*

S A U D I

ARABIA ⭐**RIYADH**

ABU DHABI ⭐

Suhar

As Sib ⭐ **MUSCAT**

Jordan

Medina

Tropic of Cancer

**UNITED ARAB
EMIRATES**

'Ibri

Saudi Arabia

Jedda

Mecca

At Taif

P E N I N S U L A

A R A B I A N

Arabian Sea

United Arab
Emirates

The dromedary is
used for milk, meat
and to carry heavy
loads. These camels are
well suited to desert life
and can go for many days
without drinking water.

Did you know?

◇ The world's
earliest civilizations
developed in
Mesopotamia,
which is now
Iraq.

*AR RUB' AL KHALI
(EMPTY QUARTER)*

O M A N

Abha

Salalah

Y E M E N

SANA ⭐

Oman

Hodeida

Al Mukalla

Ta'izz

*Socotra
(to Yemen)*

Yemen

To find out more about Southwest Asia go to:
www.scholastic.ca/atlas

Aden

Bab el Mandeb

Gulf of Aden

0   200   400 kilometres

0   200   400 miles

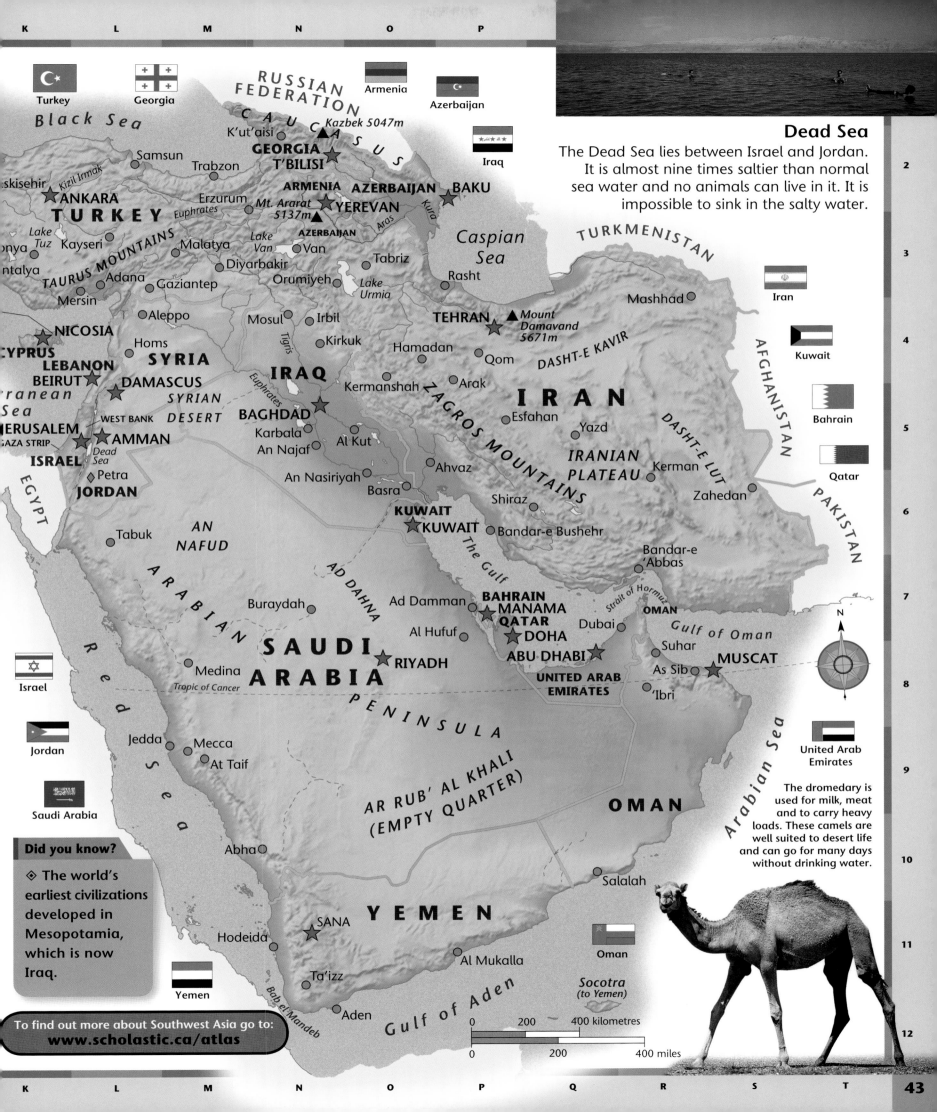

Central Asia

ASIA

The Pamirs, in the southeast of this region, form the second-highest mountain range in the world. Mountains also cover most of Kyrgyzstan and Tajikistan and much of Afghanistan. Kazakhstan has open grasslands, and further south in Uzbekistan and Turkmenistan there is a lot of sandy desert. Central Asia is land-locked, which means that it is cut off from the sea, although it has a huge inland lake called the Caspian Sea. This area gets very little rain, and winters and summers have extreme temperatures. There are few large cities and most people live in rural areas. Most of the farming is around the fertile river valleys at the base of the mountains and in Kazakhstan. The main crops include cotton, peaches, melons and apricots. Central Asia has large deposits of oil, coal and natural gas, and minerals such as iron and copper. Industries are mostly traditional ones, and some areas specialize in making carpets and leather goods.

Country File

Afghanistan

Kazakhstan

Kyrgyzstan

Tajikistan

Turkmenistan

Uzbekistan

Did you know?

◈ There are huge reserves of coal in Central Asia. It is used mostly to fuel power stations.

Ural'sk ○

RUSSIAN FEDERATION

Ural

Caspian Depression

Atyrau ○

Aktau ○

Caspian Sea

Turkmenbasy ○

Balkanabat ○

Did you know?

◈ The Caspian Sea, in the west, is the largest saltwater lake in the world. It takes up an area of 371,000 sq km.

Aral Sea

The Aral Sea once covered 68,000 square kilometres. But since 1960, it has shrunk to a quarter of its size because water from rivers that flow into the lake is being diverted to use for irrigation. Old ships that used to float on the lake are now sitting on dry land.

Samarqand

One of the oldest cities in Central Asia is Samarqand, which contains some of the finest buildings in this area. They include several Islamic schools called madrasahs. Shirdar madrasah, shown here, was built in the early 1600s. It is decorated with millions of tiles.

Snow leopard

The snow leopard lives high in the mountains of Central Asia. This big cat has very thick fur, which can be up to 10 centimetres long.

6

7

8

9

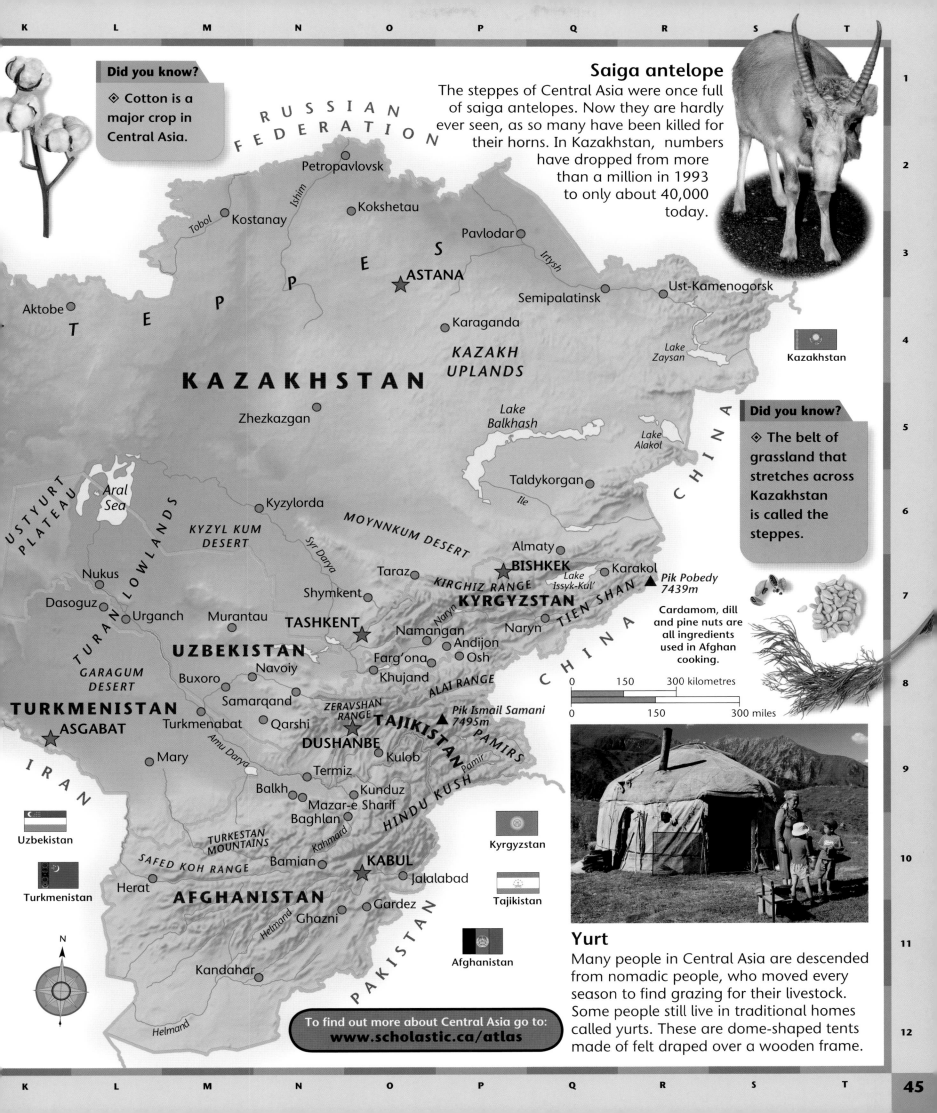

Did you know?

◈ Cotton is a major crop in Central Asia.

R U S S I A N

F E D E R A T I O N

Saiga antelope

The steppes of Central Asia were once full of saiga antelopes. Now they are hardly ever seen, as so many have been killed for their horns. In Kazakhstan, numbers have dropped from more than a million in 1993 to only about 40,000 today.

Petropavlovsk

Ishim

Tobol Kostanay Kokshetau

Pavlodar

S Irtysh

Aktobe

T E P P E S

ASTANA

Semipalatinsk Ust-Kamenogorsk

Karaganda

KAZAKH UPLANDS

Lake Zaysan

Kazakhstan

K A Z A K H S T A N

Zhezkazgan

Lake Balkhash

Lake Alakol

C H I N A

Did you know?

◈ The belt of grassland that stretches across Kazakhstan is called the steppes.

USTYURT PLATEAU

Aral Sea

Kyzylorda

KYZYL KUM DESERT

Syr Darya

MOYNNKUM DESERT

Taldykorgan

Ile

Almaty

Nukus

TURAN LOWLANDS

Dasoguz

Urganch Murantau

Taraz

KIRGHIZ RANGE

BISHKEK

Lake Issyk-Kul'

Karakol

Pik Pobedy 7439m

TIEN SHAN

Cardamom, dill and pine nuts are all ingredients used in Afghan cooking.

Shymkent

TASHKENT

Namangan

Naryn

KYRGYZSTAN

Naryn Andijon Osh

U Z B E K I S T A N

Farg'ona

GARAGUM DESERT

Buxoro Navoiy

Khujand

ALAI RANGE

C H I N A

0 150 300 kilometres

0 150 300 miles

T U R K M E N I S T A N

Samarqand

ZERAVSHAN RANGE

Pik Ismail Samani 7495m

Qarshi

TAJIKISTAN

PAMIRS

ASGABAT Turkmenabat

DUSHANBE Kulob

Amu Darya

Pamir

Mary

Termiz

Uzbekistan

I R A N

Balkh Kunduz

Mazar-e Sharif

Baghlan

HINDU KUSH

Kyrgyzstan

TURKESTAN MOUNTAINS

Kahmard

Turkmenistan

SAFED KOH RANGE

Bamian

KABUL

Jalalabad

Tajikistan

Herat

A F G H A N I S T A N

Gardez

Ghazni

Helmand

Afghanistan

Kandahar

N

P A K I S T A N

Helmand

To find out more about Central Asia go to: **www.scholastic.ca/atlas**

Yurt

Many people in Central Asia are descended from nomadic people, who moved every season to find grazing for their livestock. Some people still live in traditional homes called yurts. These are dome-shaped tents made of felt draped over a wooden frame.

South Asia

ASIA

The population of India is the second-biggest in the world. There are now about 1.1 billion people living in India.

Country File

Bangladesh

Bhutan

India

Maldives

Nepal

Pakistan

Sri Lanka

This area is also called the Indian subcontinent. South Asia is separated from the rest of Asia by the towering peaks of the Himalayas. The tops of these mountains are always covered in snow. In the south there are lush tropical rainforests, and in the west are huge areas of desert. India has a typical monsoon climate. From March to June it is hot and dry. The wet season is from June to September, when large amounts of rain fall, often causing floods. October to February is cool and dry. Over one-fifth of the world's population lives in this area. After centuries of invasion and occupation, people have a rich variety of cultures and religions, and thousands of languages are spoken. Nearly two-thirds of the population work in agriculture, although most farmers grow only enough for their family. Rice grows in the wetter areas of the east and west, and millet and corn grow on higher areas inland. Tea is an important crop, especially in southwest India and Sri Lanka.

Pakistan

IRAN

CENTRAL MAKR RANGE

Did you know?

◈ Bangladesh is one of the most densely populated countries in the world, and its population is one of the poorest. Most people survive by growing their own food.

Bollywood

Filmmaking in India is a huge industry and it is known as "Bollywood." The films often contain spectacular song-and-dance routines, with expert fight scenes and beautiful heroes and heroines. Bollywood is based in the city of Mumbai, which used to be called Bombay.

Did you know?

◈ The River Ganges is sacred to people who follow the Hindu religion, and it is worshipped as a goddess.

A cobra rears up and spreads its hood when it is alarmed.

Taj Mahal

The Mughal emperor Shah Jahan built the beautiful Taj Mahal in Agra, India, in memory of his favourite wife, Mumtaz Mahal. It took 22 years to build and was finished in 1648. The Taj Mahal consists of four buildings, one of which is a tomb containing the bodies of Shah Jahan and his wife.

Tea plantations

Sri Lanka and parts of India have the ideal climate for growing tea. Only the youngest tea leaves are picked. These are then wilted, oxidized, rolled and dried to produce the tea that we use to make the popular drink.

K L M N O P Q R S T

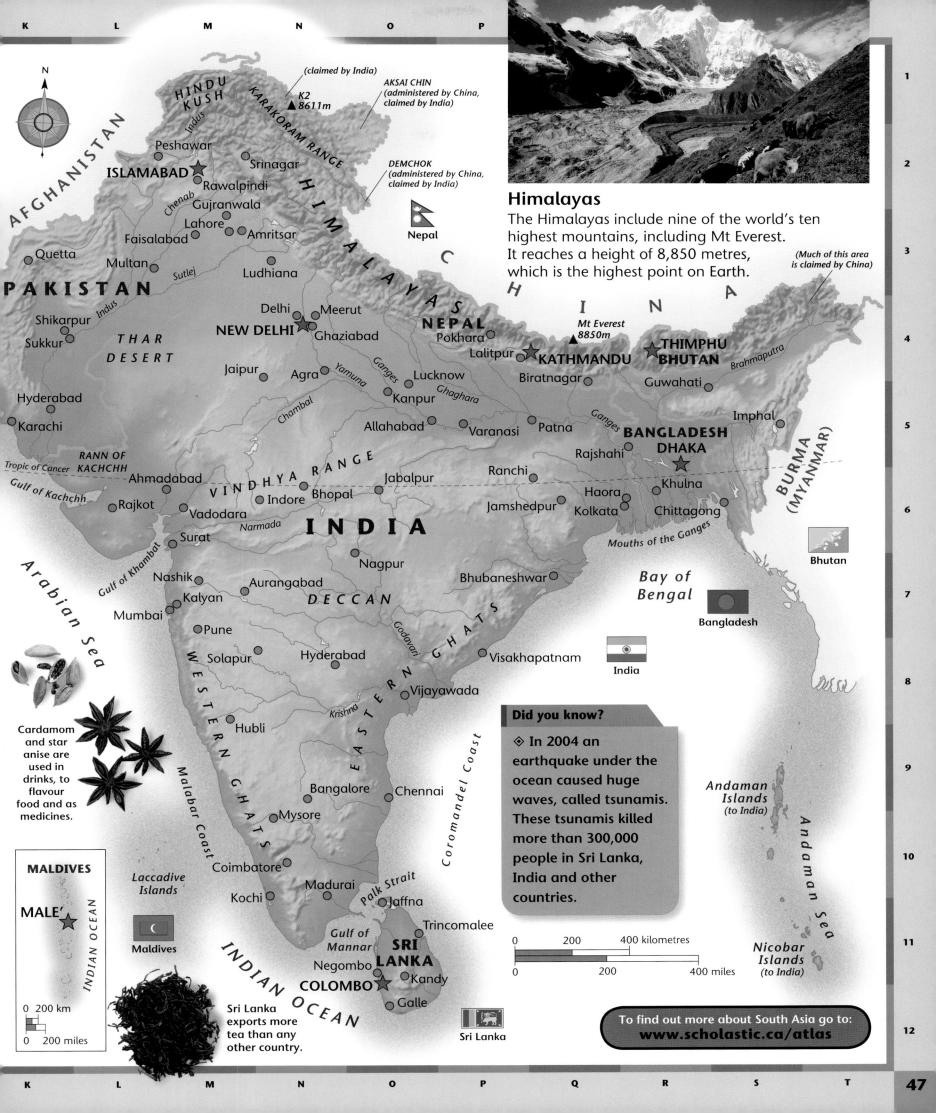

AFGHANISTAN

HINDU KUSH

KARAKORAM RANGE

Indus

(claimed by India)
K2
▲ 8611m

AKSAI CHIN
(administered by China,
claimed by India)

DEMCHOK
(administered by China,
claimed by India)

Peshawar

Srinagar

ISLAMABAD ★

Rawalpindi

Chenab

Gujranwala

Lahore

Faisalabad
Amritsar

Quetta

Multan

Sutlej

Ludhiana

Nepal

PAKISTAN

Shikarpur

Indus

Sukkur

THAR
DESERT

Delhi
Meerut

NEW DELHI ★
Ghaziabad

NEPAL

Pokhara

Lalitpur ★ KATHMANDU

THIMPHU ★
BHUTAN

Jaipur

Agra

Yamuna

Ganges

Lucknow

Biratnagar

Guwahati

Kanpur

Ghaghara

Hyderabad

Chambal

Allahabad

Varanasi

Patna

Ganges

BANGLADESH

Imphal

Karachi

RANN OF
KACHCHH

Tropic of Cancer

DHAKA

Gulf of Kachchh

Ahmadabad

VINDHYA RANGE

Jabalpur

Ranchi

Rajshahi

Khulna

BURMA
(MYANMAR)

Rajkot

Indore
Bhopal

Jamshedpur

Haora

Kolkata
Chittagong

Bhutan

Vadodara

Narmada

INDIA

Surat

Gulf of Khambat

Nagpur

Mouths of the Ganges

Nashik

Bhubaneshwar

Bay of
Bengal

Bangladesh

Kalyan

Aurangabad

DECCAN

Mumbai

Pune

Godavari

India

Solapur

Hyderabad

EASTERN GHATS

Cardamom
and star
anise are
used in
drinks, to
flavour
food and as
medicines.

WESTERN GHATS

Hubli

Krishna

Vijayawada

Visakhapatnam

Coromandel Coast

Did you know?

❖ In 2004 an
earthquake under the
ocean caused huge
waves, called tsunamis.
These tsunamis killed
more than 300,000
people in Sri Lanka,
India and other
countries.

Andaman
Islands
(to India)

Malabar Coast

Bangalore

Chennai

Mysore

Andaman Sea

MALDIVES

Laccadive
Islands

Coimbatore

MALE' ★

INDIAN OCEAN

Madurai

Kochi

Palk Strait

Jaffna

Trincomalee

0   200
400 kilometres

0   200
400 miles

Nicobar
Islands
(to India)

Maldives

0 200 km

0 200 miles

Gulf of
Mannar

Negombo

SRI
LANKA

COLOMBO ★

Kandy

Sri Lanka
exports more
tea than any
other country.

INDIAN OCEAN

Galle

Sri Lanka

Himalayas

The Himalayas include nine of the world's ten
highest mountains, including Mt Everest.
It reaches a height of 8,850 metres,
which is the highest point on Earth.

(Much of this area
is claimed by China)

Mt Everest
▲ 8850m

Brahmaputra

To find out more about South Asia go to:
www.scholastic.ca/atlas

47

East Asia

ASIA

A large part of East Asia has a landscape of high mountains, desert or steppe land. In the southeast the land changes from mountains to wide river valleys and open plains. To the east is Japan, which has a rugged, mountainous landscape. Japan is one of the richest nations in the world. It does not have many natural resources, so it imports them. Japan is well known for making advanced electronic equipment. It is also a world leader in vehicle manufacturing. China and South Korea now have strong economies.

Country File

China

Japan

Mongolia

North Korea

South Korea

Taiwan

Did you know?

◈ Only about 15% of the land in Japan is suitable for farming, but Japan grows enough rice to feed its population.

KAZAKHSTAN

ALTAI MOUNTAINS

DZUNGARIAN BASIN

KYRGYZSTAN

TIEN SHAN

Urumqi

TAJIKISTAN

TARIM BASIN

PAKISTAN

(Claimed by India)

K2 ▲ 8611m

TAKLA MAKAN DESERT

ALTUN SHAN

QILIAN SHAN

KUNLUN MOUNTAINS

QAIDAM BASIN

(Administered by China, claimed by India)

(Administered by China, claimed by India)

INDIA

PLATEAU OF TIBET

C H

HIMALAYAS

NEPAL

Salween

T i b e t

Brahmaputra

Lhasa

China

Mt Everest 8850m

BHUTAN

INDIA

BURMA

Mekong

LAO

Great Wall of China

The Great Wall of China is one of the largest structures in the world. It starts near the Chinese coast and stretches inland, across northern China, for over 6,400 kilometres. This huge wall was started in 220 BCE and took 10 years to build. It was made to keep out invaders from the north, such as the Mongols.

Did you know?

◈ **The official language of China is Mandarin. More people speak this than any other language in the world.**

◈ **More than one-fifth of the world's population lives in China.**

Traditional herbal medicine, such as these wolf berries, has been used in China for over 4,500 years.

Giant panda

These are among the most endangered animals in the world. There are only about 1,600 left in the wild. Pandas are classified as carnivores (meat eaters), but 99 per cent of their diet is bamboo. Pandas live in thick bamboo forests in central China and spend about 14 hours a day eating!

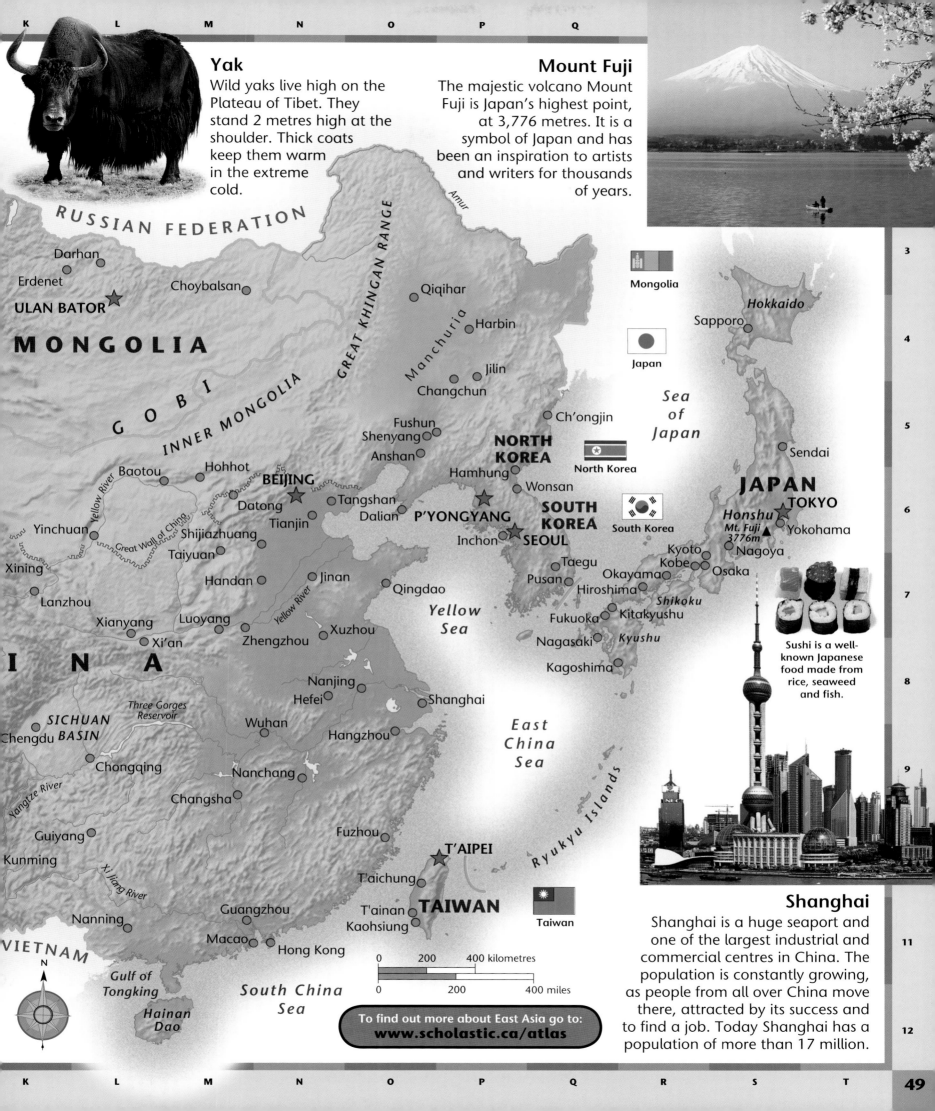

Yak
Wild yaks live high on the Plateau of Tibet. They stand 2 metres high at the shoulder. Thick coats keep them warm in the extreme cold.

Mount Fuji
The majestic volcano Mount Fuji is Japan's highest point, at 3,776 metres. It is a symbol of Japan and has been an inspiration to artists and writers for thousands of years.

RUSSIAN FEDERATION

Amur

Darhan

Erdenet

Choybalsan

ULAN BATOR

M O N G O L I A

G O B I

INNER MONGOLIA

GREAT KHINGAN RANGE

Qiqihar

Manchuria

Harbin

Jilin

Changchun

Mongolia

Hokkaido

Sapporo

Ch'ongjin

Sea of Japan

Fushun
Shenyang
Anshan

NORTH KOREA

North Korea

Hamhung

Wonsan

Sendai

JAPAN
TOKYO

Yellow River

Baotou

Hohhot

BEIJING

Datong

Tangshan

Dalian

P'YONGYANG

SOUTH KOREA

South Korea

Honshu
Mt. Fuji
3776m ▲

Yokohama

Yinchuan

Great Wall of China

Shijiazhuang

Tianjin

Inchon

SEOUL

Kyoto
Kobe
Nagoya
Osaka

Xining

Taiyuan

Handan

Jinan

Taegu

Pusan

Okayama
Hiroshima

Lanzhou

Xianyang

Luoyang

Yellow River

Qingdao

Yellow Sea

Shikoku

Fukuoka
Kitakyushu

Xi'an

Zhengzhou

Xuzhou

Nagasaki

Kyushu

Sushi is a well-known Japanese food made from rice, seaweed and fish.

I N A

Kagoshima

Nanjing

Hefei

Shanghai

SICHUAN BASIN

Three Gorges Reservoir

Wuhan

Hangzhou

East China Sea

Chengdu

Chongqing

Nanchang

Changsha

Ryukyu Islands

Guiyang

Xi Jiang River

Fuzhou

T'AIPEI

Kunming

T'aichung

Nanning

Guangzhou

T'ainan

TAIWAN

Taiwan

Kaohsiung

Macao

Hong Kong

VIETNAM

N

Gulf of Tongking

Hainan Dao

South China Sea

Yangtze River

0   200   400 kilometres

0   200   400 miles

To find out more about East Asia go to:
www.scholastic.ca/atlas

Shanghai
Shanghai is a huge seaport and one of the largest industrial and commercial centres in China. The population is constantly growing, as people from all over China move there, attracted by its success and to find a job. Today Shanghai has a population of more than 17 million.

3
4
5
6
7
8
9
11
12

K L M N O P Q R S T

49

Country File

Brunei

Burma (Myanmar)

Cambodia

East Timor

Indonesia

Laos

Malaysia

Philippines

Singapore

Thailand

Vietnam

Did you know?

◈ The red gemstones called rubies are mined in Burma. Burmese rubies are known as the finest rubies in the world.

Did you know?

◈ Siamese cats originally came from Thailand.

Burma

Hkakabo Razi 5885m ▲

Laos

Vietnam

INDIA

BANGLADESH

Chindwin

Irrawaddy

Tropic of Cancer

CHINA

BURMA

Mandalay

SHAN PLATEAU

Meiktila

Taunggyi

Sittwe

Magwe

NAYPYIDAW

LAOS

HA NOI

Hai Phong

Nam Dinh

Louangphabang

Vinh

Prome

Bay of Bengal

Salween

Chiang Mai

VIENTIANE

VIETNAM

Yangon

Pegu

Bassein

Moulmein

Udon Thani

ANNAMESE CORDILLERA

Hué

Da Nang

Mouths of the Irrawaddy

Gulf of Martaban

THAILAND

Nakhon Ratchasima

Mekong

Pakxé

Orangutan

These mammals are the only great apes in Asia and they are critically endangered. Their habitat is being destroyed and they are hunted for their young, which are sold as pets. Orangutans eat mostly fruit, but they also feed on leaves, shoots, insects and occasionally small animals and eggs.

Thailand

Tavoy

BANGKOK

Chon Buri

Angor Wat

Tonle Sap

Nha Trang

Batdambang

CAMBODIA

Malaysia

Mergui Archipelago

PHNOM PENH

Gulf of Thailand

Bien Hoa

Ho Chi Minh

My Tho

Rach Gia

Can Tho

Did you know?

◈ Angkor Wat in Cambodia is the world's largest religious monument. It dates back to 1113.

Ko Samui

Phuket

Hat Yai

Cambodia

South China Sea

Banda Aceh

Kuala Terengganu

Singapore

Singapore is a city-state made up of a main island (Singapore Island) and 62 other islands. It is the biggest port in Southeast Asia, one of the world's main oil-refining centres and a world leader in shipbuilding and repair. Singapore also has a thriving technology industry.

Ipoh

Medan

KUALA LUMPUR

MALAY

Natuna Islands

Lake Toba

Klang

Johor Bahru

Natuna Sea

Kuching

Equator

Pekanbaru

SINGAPORE

Pontianak

Did you know?

◈ In Singapore it is illegal to sell chewing gum or to drop litter.

Padang

Jambi

Bangka

Mentawai Islands

Great

Bengkulu

Palembang

I N

Bandarlampung

JAKARTA

Tangerang

Bogor

Bandung

Semarang

Java

Singapore

Yogyakarta

Paddy fields

People grow rice throughout Southeast Asia. Rice needs plenty of water and heat so this area's climate is ideal. Rice fields are called paddy fields. Each field has a low wall so that it can be flooded with water. On steep slopes the paddy fields are built in terraces.

0 — 250 — 500 kilometres

0 — 250 — 500 miles

Andaman Sea

Malay Peninsula

Isthmus of Kra

Strait of Malacca

BARISAN MOUNTAINS

Sumatra

INDIAN OCEAN

Southeast Asia

ASIA

Much of Southeast Asia is mountainous and covered in thick forest. This area has a tropical monsoon climate: half of the year is wet and half is dry. Most of the people live in the river valleys, on the fertile plains of the mainland or around the coasts of the islands. Some islands have no people living on them, but others, such as Java, have a big population. People in this area are from many different cultures. They follow many religions and speak hundreds of languages. The main industries are processing raw materials, such as oil, minerals, timber and food. Recently, the manufacturing of electronic goods and computers has increased.

Buddhism

One of the main religions in this area is Buddhism. Like many Buddhist temples, this one is guarded by statues of lions at the entrance.

Lemongrass, lime and cilantro are important ingredients in Southeast Asian cooking.

Komodo dragon

This is the world's largest lizard. It grows up to 3 metres long. Komodo dragons live on the Lesser Sunda Islands. Their teeth are serrated and their mouths are full of deadly bacteria. They are fierce predators and eat anything that they can overpower.

N

Did you know?

◈ The sultan of Brunei has the largest palace in the world.

Did you know?

◈ Indonesia is a group of 17,500 islands. This is called an "archipelago."

Unusual carved wooden masks like this one are worn by professional dancers in Indonesia.

Philippines

Brunei

East Timor

Indonesia

Luzon
Baguio
MANILA
Philippine Sea
Mindoro
PHILIPPINES
Samar
Panay
Bacolod   Cebu
Negros
Palawan
Sulu Sea
Cagayan de Oro
Mindanao
Zamboanga
Davao
BANDAR SERI BEGAWAN
Mount Kinabalu 4101m
Sandakan
BRUNEI
Kota Kinabalu
Sulu Archipelago
Celebes Sea
PACIFIC OCEAN
A S I A
Borneo
Manado
Halmahera
Equator
Samarinda
Makassar Strait
Palu
Molucca Sea
Jayapura
Balikpapan
Sulawesi
Papua
Sunda Islands
Ceram
Puncak Jaya ▲ 4884m
CENTRAL RANGE
I N D O N E S I A
Banjarmasin
Kendari
Buru
Ambon
PAPUA NEW GUINEA
Java Sea
Makassar
Banda Sea
Aru Islands
Surabaya
Flores Sea
Arafura Sea
Malang   Bali   Lesser Sunda Islands
Denpasar   Mataram   Flores   DILI
Lombok   Sumbawa   EAST TIMOR
Sumba   Kupang   Timor   Timor Sea

To find out more about Southeast Asia go to:
www.scholastic.ca/atlas

Australia
OCEANIA AND THE PACIFIC ISLANDS

This massive country is mostly desert, which is so hot and dry that it is not suitable for farming or for people to live there. The wildest, driest and emptiest parts of the Australian desert are sometimes called the outback. Most of the 20 million people in Australia live in towns along the coast, such as Brisbane, Melbourne and Sydney in the east and Perth in the southwest. The first inhabitants of this continent were the Aboriginal Australians. Today most Australians are descended from European people who migrated there from the 18th century onwards. Australia has one of the world's biggest mining industries. Copper, gold, coal and opals are all mined there. Other important Australian industries include tourism and winemaking.

Did you know?

◈ The world's longest fence is in Australia. It is 5,320 km long and was built to keep dingos away from sheep.

97 per cent of all opals are found in Australia.

INDIAN OCEAN

KIMBERLEY PLATEAU

Broome

GREAT SANDY DESERT

Port Hedland

Dampier

HAMERSLEY RANGE

GIBSON DESERT

Lake Mackay

Tropic of Capricorn

A U

WESTERN AUSTRALIA

GREAT VICTORIA DESERT

Geraldton

Kalgoorlie

NULLARBO

Perth ☆
Fremantle
Mandurah
Bunbury

Cape Leeuwin

Albany

Great A

SOUTHERN

0   200   400 kilometres
0   200   400 miles

Uluru

The magnificent rock called Uluru is the top of an enormous sandstone hill that is buried beneath the desert in Northern Territory. It is also known as Ayers Rock. This is the world's biggest single rock. Uluru rises nearly 350 metres above the surrounding land and it is 9.4 kilometres around the base. This ancient rock is a sacred place for many Aboriginal Australians.

Kangaroo

Kangaroos are mammals called marsupials. The females carry their young in a pouch. Other marsupials in Australia are wallabies, possums and the koala. The only egg-laying mammals – the platypus and echidna – also live in Australia. They are called monotremes.

To find out more about Australia go to:
www.scholastic.ca/atlas

Did you know?

◇ Australia is the only country that is also a continent on its own.

Arafura Sea

Melville Island

★ Darwin

ARNHEM LAND

N

Gulf of Carpentaria

Cape York

CAPE YORK PENINSULA

BARKLY TABLELAND

TANAMI DESERT

NORTHERN TERRITORY

Coral Sea

Cairns

GREAT BARRIER REEF

Townsville

MACDONNELL RANGES

Alice Springs

QUEENSLAND

Mackay

▲ Uluru (Ayers Rock) 867m

SIMPSON DESERT

Rockhampton

Gladstone

T R A L I A

SOUTH AUSTRALIA

Lake Eyre North

Hervey Bay

Maroochydore-Mooloolaba

Sunshine Coast

★ Brisbane

Gold Coast

Coober Pedy

Lake Torrens

Lake Frome

Lake Gairdner

FLINDERS RANGES

Darling River

NEW SOUTH WALES

GREAT DIVIDING RANGE

Coffs Harbour

AIN

Broken Hill

Port Macquarie

lian Bight

CEAN

Adelaide ★

Mildura

Bathurst

Newcastle

★ Sydney

Wollongong

Kangaroo Island

Wagga Wagga

Murray River

Albury

Nowra

★ CANBERRA

Mount Kosciuszko 2228m ▲

AUSTRALIAN ALPS

AUSTRALIAN CAPITAL TERRITORY

Bendigo

VICTORIA

Ballarat

Geelong

★ Melbourne

Bass Strait

Launceston

TASMANIA

★ Hobart

PACIFIC OCEAN

Australia

Great Barrier Reef

The Great Barrier Reef is made up of over 2,800 coral reefs and is home to more than 1,500 species of fish. It covers an enormous area – 350,000 square kilometres.

Koala

The koala lives in eucalyptus trees and eats the leaves. Many of these trees are being cut down to make more space for roads and buildings. Koalas are now endangered animals.

Did you know?

◇ The inland taipan has the strongest venom of any land snake. The venom in one bite could kill 100 people.

Sydney Opera House

Sydney is the biggest and oldest city in Australia, and the Sydney Opera House is one of the most famous buildings in the world. Over 100 million people have visited it.

Pacific Islands

OCEANIA AND THE PACIFIC ISLANDS

There are thousands of islands in the Pacific Ocean. People from many cultures live there, speaking many languages. The islands are traditionally divided into these groups: Melanesia, Micronesia and Polynesia. The earliest people in this region settled on the island of New Guinea over 40,000 years ago. In the 19th century, the islands were colonized by Europeans, who brought their own cultures, languages and religions. Most of the islands are now part of independent countries. They rely on agriculture fishing for their income. The islands also export copra, which comes from coconuts. It is made into coconut oil, which is used in soap and cosmetics.

Country File

- Fiji
- Kiribati
- Marshall Islands
- Micronesia
- Nauru
- Palau
- Papua New Guinea
- Samoa
- Solomon Islands
- Tonga
- Tuvalu
- Vanuatu

Onions, limes, ginger, garlic and lemon juice are all traditional ingredients of many south Pacific island dishes.

Did you know?

◇ Nauru, in Micronesia, is the is the world's smallest republic. It has an area of only 21 sq km.

Tropic of Cancer

NORTHERN MARIANA ISLANDS (to US)

Marshall Islan

Micronesia

GUAM (to US)
HAGATNA

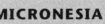
M i c r o

Palau

Yap
Babeldaob

MICRONESIA

Chuuk Islands
PALIKIR
Pohnpei

OREOR
PALAU

Caroline Islands
Ko

Equator

Papua New Guinea

INDONESIA

M
e

PAPUA NEW GUINEA
▲ Mount Wilhelm 4509m
New Britain

PORT MORESBY

Guadalcanal
HONIARA

SO
IS

Coral Sea

Solomon Islands

AUSTRALIA

N
CALEDON (to Fra

Tropic of Caprico

Vanuatu

Fishing

The people of the Pacific islands fish mainly to feed themselves, but many fish are also caught in the northern Pacific by big fishing boats from Japan, South Korea, Taiwan and the USA. Tuna is a prized fish, and the finest tuna can sell for thousands of dollars per fish, especially in Japan. Today much of the commercial fishing of tuna is done using long fishing lines instead of nets.

Doria's tree kangaroo

Nine of the 11 species of tree kangaroo live in the rainforest on the island of New Guinea. The other two live in Australia. Doria's tree kangaroo is the largest one, weighing up to 13 kilograms. Like all kangaroos, it is a marsupial.

Did you know?

◇ Most of the Pacific Islands were formed by volcanoes.

Papua New Guinea

New Guinea is the second-largest island in the world, and Papua New Guinea takes up the eastern half, as well as several smaller islands. About 80 per cent of the population lives in groups in the countryside. People live as they have done for many hundreds of years, with traditional ways of life, customs and beliefs.

Did you know?

◇ Papua New Guinea has more than 820 living languages.

◇ The coconut tree is called "the tree of life" by many islanders because every part of it is used or eaten.

Cyclones

The Pacific islands suffer from cyclones every year. These strong winds blow at more than 120 kilometres per hour and can cause serious damage. In other parts of the world they are called typhoons or hurricanes. Palm trees can bend in the wind and survive cyclones.

Farming

Many Pacific islands are mountainous but people are able to grow some food crops along the coast. Coconuts, sweet potatoes and bananas all grow well in the hot, humid climate of the Pacific. Cocoa and coffee are important crops in Papua New Guinea.

Green turtle

These endangered turtles live in warm waters all around the Pacific. They can reach 1.5 metres in length. The adults feed on sea grasses and algae, but the young eat jellyfish, shellfish and sponges.

The International Date Line is an imaginary line that separates two calendar days. This means that the date to the east of the line is always one day ahead of the date to the west of the line.

Did you know?

◈ In Papua New Guinea a language called Tok Pisin has developed, so that different communities can speak to each other.

Polynesia

The beautiful island of Bora-Bora is in French Polynesia, a territory of France. Bora-Bora is one of the main tourist destinations of French Polynesia. Its highest peak is Mount Otemanu, which is 727 metres high.

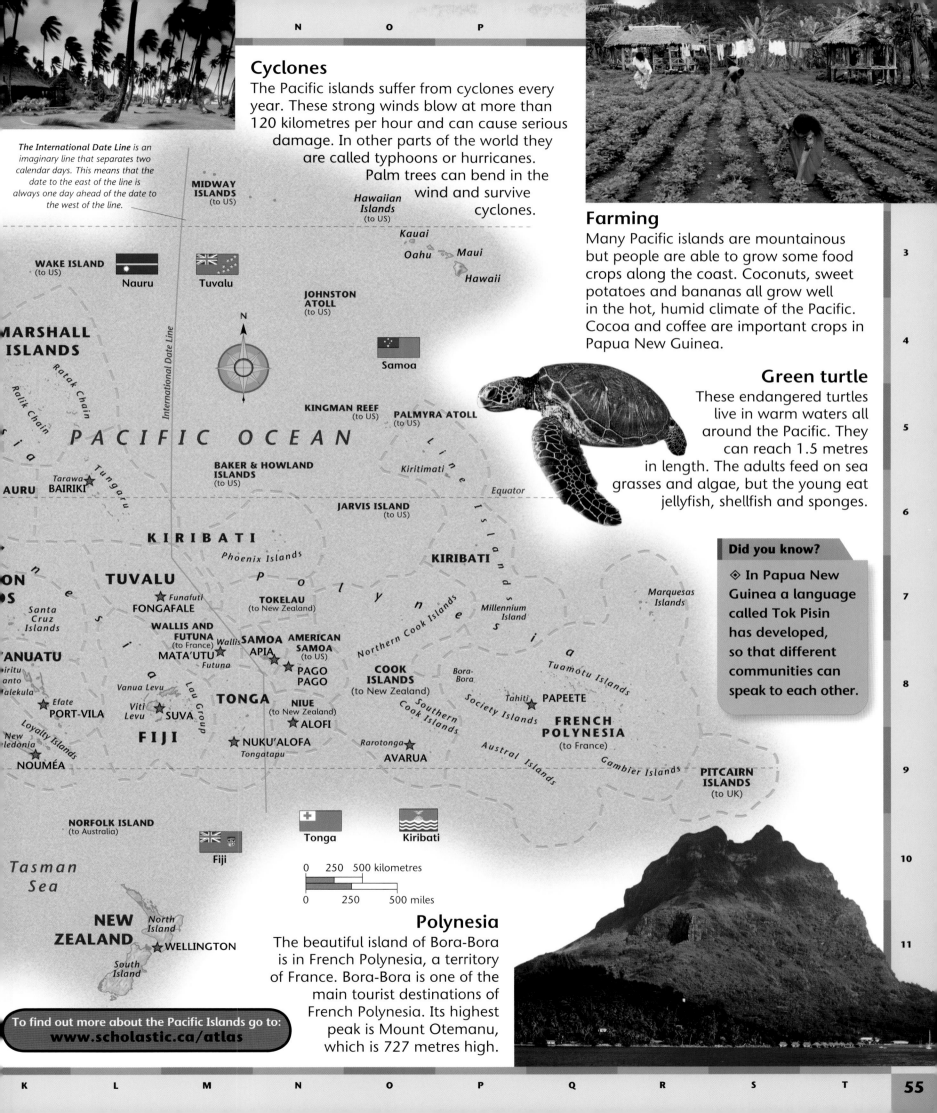

MIDWAY ISLANDS (to US)

Hawaiian Islands (to US)
Kauai
Oahu   Maui
Hawaii

WAKE ISLAND (to US)
Nauru
Tuvalu

JOHNSTON ATOLL (to US)

Samoa

MARSHALL ISLANDS

Ratak Chain
Ralik Chain

International Date Line

N

PACIFIC OCEAN

KINGMAN REEF (to US)   PALMYRA ATOLL (to US)

Line Islands

BAKER & HOWLAND ISLANDS (to US)
Kiritimati

Tarawa BAIRIKI   Tungaru
AURU

Equator

JARVIS ISLAND (to US)

KIRIBATI

Phoenix Islands   KIRIBATI

TUVALU   P o l y n e s i a

Santa Cruz Islands

★ Funafuti
FONGAFALE

TOKELAU (to New Zealand)

Millennium Island

Marquesas Islands

WALLIS AND FUTUNA (to France)   Wallis SAMOA AMERICAN SAMOA (to US)
MATA'UTU   APIA
Futuna   PAGO PAGO

COOK ISLANDS (to New Zealand)

Northern Cook Islands

Bora-Bora

Tuamotu Islands

ANUATU
iritu
anto
alekula

Vanua Levu

TONGA

NIUE (to New Zealand)
★ ALOFI

Society Islands   Tahiti PAPEETE

Southern Cook Islands

FRENCH POLYNESIA (to France)

Efate PORT-VILA
Viti Levu SUVA

Loyalty Islands
New ledonia
NOUMÉA

FIJI

Lau Group

★ NUKU'ALOFA
Tongatapu

Rarotonga ★
AVARUA

Austral Islands

Gambier Islands

PITCAIRN ISLANDS (to UK)

NORFOLK ISLAND (to Australia)

Tonga   Kiribati

Fiji

0   250   500 kilometres

0   250   500 miles

Tasman Sea

NEW ZEALAND   North Island
★ WELLINGTON
South Island

To find out more about the Pacific Islands go to:
www.scholastic.ca/atlas

New Zealand

OCEANIA AND THE PACIFIC ISLANDS

Country File

New Zealand

This country in the south Pacific Ocean is about one quarter the size of Ontario. It consists of two main islands – North Island and South Island – and several smaller islands. New Zealand is known for its spectacular scenery. The landscape includes mountains, volcanoes, long sandy beaches, deep fjords and lush rainforests. It has cool, wet winters and warm, wet summers. New Zealand is one of the world's least populated countries, with 4.25 million people. The first people to settle there about 1,000 years ago were the Polynesians. They became known as the Maoris. For the past 160 years people have migrated there from many countries. Tourism, fishing and high-tech manufacturing are important industries.

Auckland

The largest city in New Zealand is Auckland. About one-third of the population lives there. More than 60 per cent of residents are descended from Europeans, and 11 per cent are Maori. Nobody in Auckland lives more than half an hour away from a beach.

Did you know?

❖ Almost one-third of New Zealand is covered by forest. Many of the forests contain unusual species of trees that are found only on these islands, such as kauri trees, which are some of the oldest trees on Earth.

This wooden Maori Tiki carving represents the first man. Tiki carvings are thought of as powerful good luck symbols.

Whale-watching

One of the best places to see whales and dolphins in the wild is near the town of Kaikoura, on the east coast of South Island. New Zealand's whales, dolphins and seals are protected, and visitors from all over the world travel to Kaikoura to see them.

Tasman Sea

Westport

Greymouth

South Island

Aoraki/
Mount Cook
3754m ▲

Haast

Ashburton

Milford
Sound

SOUTHERN ALPS

Timaru

Wanaka

Canterbury Bight

Lake Wakatipu

Waitaki

Queenstown

Oamaru

FIORDLAND

Lake
Te Anau

Te Anau

Matoura

Clutha

Dunedin

Invercargill

Foveaux Strait

Stewart Island

Aoraki/Mount Cook

The highest mountain in New Zealand is Aoraki/ Mount Cook in the Southern Alps. It is 3,754 metres high. In Maori legend, these mountains are Aoraki and his three brothers, who are the sons of the Sky Father. They were stranded in their canoe and were frozen by the cold south wind. Their canoe became South Island.

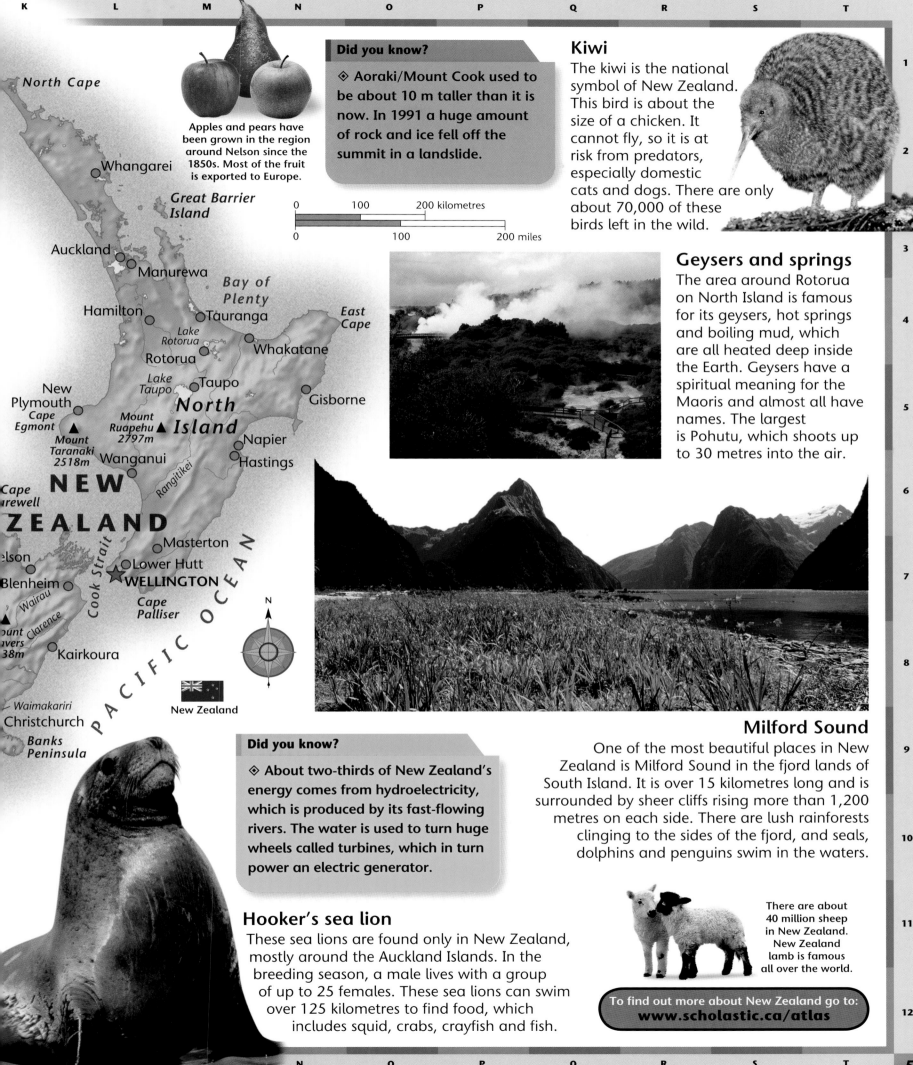

North Cape

Apples and pears have been grown in the region around Nelson since the 1850s. Most of the fruit is exported to Europe.

Kiwi

The kiwi is the national symbol of New Zealand. This bird is about the size of a chicken. It cannot fly, so it is at risk from predators, especially domestic cats and dogs. There are only about 70,000 of these birds left in the wild.

Whangarei

Great Barrier Island

0   100   200 kilometres

0   100   200 miles

Auckland

Manurewa

Bay of Plenty

Hamilton

East Cape

Tauranga

Lake Rotorua

Whakatane

Rotorua

Lake Taupo

Taupo

New Plymouth

North Island

Gisborne

Cape Egmont

Mount Ruapehu 2797m

Mount Taranaki 2518m

Napier

Wanganui

Rangitikei

Hastings

Geysers and springs

The area around Rotorua on North Island is famous for its geysers, hot springs and boiling mud, which are all heated deep inside the Earth. Geysers have a spiritual meaning for the Maoris and almost all have names. The largest is Pohutu, which shoots up to 30 metres into the air.

Cape arewell

NEW

ZEALAND

elson

Masterton

Cook Strait

Lower Hutt

WELLINGTON

Blenheim

Wairau

Cape Palliser

Clarence

ount avers 38m

Kairkoura

PACIFIC OCEAN

N

New Zealand

Waimakariri

Christchurch

Banks Peninsula

Milford Sound

One of the most beautiful places in New Zealand is Milford Sound in the fjord lands of South Island. It is over 15 kilometres long and is surrounded by sheer cliffs rising more than 1,200 metres on each side. There are lush rainforests clinging to the sides of the fjord, and seals, dolphins and penguins swim in the waters.

There are about 40 million sheep in New Zealand. New Zealand lamb is famous all over the world.

Hooker's sea lion

These sea lions are found only in New Zealand, mostly around the Auckland Islands. In the breeding season, a male lives with a group of up to 25 females. These sea lions can swim over 125 kilometres to find food, which includes squid, crabs, crayfish and fish.

To find out more about New Zealand go to:
www.scholastic.ca/atlas

Arctic Circle

Bering Strait

USA
(Alaska)

Chukchi
Sea

Wrangel
Island

R U S S I A N

Limit of summer pack ice

Limit of permanent ice cap

Beaufort
Sea

East
Siberian
Sea

New
Siberian
Islands

C A N A D A

Banks
Island

A R C T I C
O C E A N

Laptev
Sea

F E D E R A T I O N

Victoria
Island

Melville
Island

Queen
Elizabeth
Islands

North Pole

Severnaya
Zemlya

Taymyr Peninsula

Ellesmere
Island

Kara
Sea

Qaanaaq

Knud
Rasmussen
Land

Wandel
Sea

Franz
Josef
Land

Novaya Zemlya

Baffin Island

Baffin
Bay

Limit of permanent ice cap

SVALBARD
(to Norway)

Davis Strait

Limit of summer pack ice

Limit of winter pack ice

Barents
Sea

Aasiat
Ilulissat
Sisimiut
Maniitsoq
NUUK

GREENLAND
(to Denmark)

Kong Christian IX Land

Greenland
Sea

North Cape

Kola
Peninsula

Gunnbjørn
Fjeld
3,700m

Ittoqqortoormiit

Norwegian
Sea

N O R W A Y

F I N L A N D

Qaqortoq

Tasiilaq

Denmark Strait

Nunap Isua

Arctic Circle

REYKJAVIK ★ ICELAND

0   400   800 kilometres

0   400   800 miles

The Arctic

ASIA, EUROPE AND NORTH AMERICA

The Arctic is a huge area with the North Pole at its
centre. It is not a continent or a country but includes
the Arctic Ocean and the most northern parts of Asia,
North America and Europe. During winter, much of the
Arctic Ocean is covered by pack ice about 4 metres thick.
During the short summers, the ice melts and the area of
pack ice shrinks. It grows again when winter returns and
temperatures drop to −60°C. Even though the climate
is cold, people have lived in the Arctic for thousands of
years. The Sami and Inuit people were originally nomads
who survived by herding animals and hunting. Today
most people live in new towns, but some still live a
traditional life.

Polar bear

There are 21–25,000 polar bears in
the Arctic. These animals are now
a threatened species. As the Arctic
pack ice continues to melt, polar
bears are finding it difficult to
hunt for food because they have
to swim so far between the bits
of ice. Many polar bears are
dying as they search for food.

Did you know?

◈ **By 2030 the
Arctic may have
ice-free summers
because so much
ice is melting
in summer and
not refreezing in
winter.**

Inuit people once lived by fishing,
herding and hunting whales, bears
and seals.

Northern lights

The *aurora borealis*, or the northern lights,
are caused by solar winds reacting with the
Earth's upper atmosphere. This colourful
effect in the sky can also be seen around
the South Pole, where it is known as the
southern lights, or *aurora australis*.

Antarctica

ANTARCTICA

This is the fifth-largest continent. It is almost one and a half times the size of Canada. Antarctica has a harsh, cold climate and is the windiest place on Earth. Almost all of Antarctica is covered with a sheet of ice. On average, the ice is 1.6 kilometres thick, and it is thousands of years old. The ice contains most of the fresh water on Earth. Under the ice, the land contains oil and other minerals, including gold, iron ore and coal. Huge blocks of ice often break off the edge of the sheet and float away as icebergs. To protect this wilderness and its wildlife, 46 nations have signed an agreement called the Antarctic Treaty. They agree not to carry out any mining or put a military station there. Antarctica is the only continent where people do not live all year round.

Cold science

Groups of scientists, tourists and explorers are allowed to visit Antarctica. Many things are studied in Antarctica, including how plants and animals can survive there.

Humpbacks and other whales visit the icy seas of Antarctica. When a whale leaps out of the water it is known as breaching.

Did you know?

◈ The weight of the ice in Antarctica has pushed the land below sea level.

Emperor penguin

The only penguins that breed in Antarctica during the bitter cold winter are emperor penguins. They weigh over 30 kilograms and are the tallest penguins, at 1.2 metres high. They walk up to 120 kilometres to their breeding grounds.

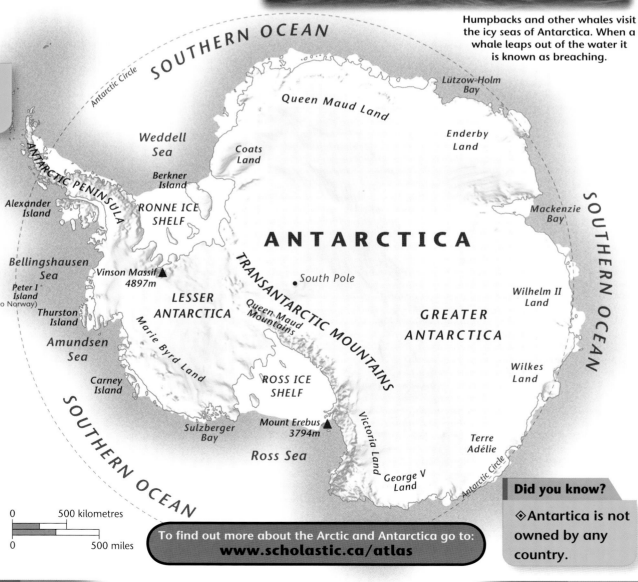

SOUTHERN OCEAN

Antarctic Circle

Queen Maud Land

Lützow-Holm Bay

Weddell Sea

Coats Land

Enderby Land

Berkner Island

ANTARCTIC PENINSULA

Alexander Island

RONNE ICE SHELF

Mackenzie Bay

ANTARCTICA

SOUTHERN OCEAN

Bellingshausen Sea

Vinson Massif ▲ 4897m

• South Pole

Wilhelm II Land

Peter I Island (to Norway)

LESSER ANTARCTICA

TRANSANTARCTIC MOUNTAINS

Queen Maud Mountains

GREATER ANTARCTICA

Thurston Island

Marie Byrd Land

Amundsen Sea

Carney Island

ROSS ICE SHELF

Wilkes Land

Sulzberger Bay

Mount Erebus ▲ 3794m

Victoria Land

Terre Adélie

Ross Sea

George V Land

Antarctic Circle

SOUTHERN OCEAN

0 — 500 kilometres

0 — 500 miles

To find out more about the Arctic and Antarctica go to:
www.scholastic.ca/atlas

Did you know?

◈ Antartica is not owned by any country.

Index to the maps

In this Atlas there is an **Index to the maps** on page 60 and a **General index** on page 68.

Place name index
The **Index to the maps** lists all the names that appear on the maps. Each name is followed by a description, its location, a page number and a grid reference number. Town names do not have a description.

place name   description   location

Anatolia *physical region* Turkey **10 D5**

page number
grid reference

To find our example "Anatolia," first go to the page shown—p. 10, then find the letter "D" and number "5" around the border of the page. Trace a line down from "D" and a line across from "5." Where the lines meet directs you to the precise square on the grid in which "Anatolia" can be found.

General index

The **General index** lists all the main topics that you can read about in this book and tells you the pages where they can be found.

Picture sources

The publisher would like to thank the following individuals and organizations for their permission to use their photographs:

Abbreviations
t = top; b = bottom; c = centre;
r = right; l = left.

Aloysius Han - www.geohavens. com for the rubies on p50; Alstom; Automobili Lamborghini SpA; CN Tower, Canada; Dickinson by Design; Ford Motor Company; International Crane Foundation, Baraboo, Wisconsin; Jumeirah International; Memories of New Zealand -www. memoriesofnz.co.nz; Saab Great Britain Ltd

Ardea: John Wombe/Auscape/ Ardea. com 53 bc

Britain on View: www.britainonview. com 34 bc

Bruce Coleman: 55 cr

Corbis: Tiziana and Gianni Baldizzone: 32 tr; Sharna Balfour; Gallo Images: 31 tr; Tom Bean: 36 bl; Fernando Bengoechea/Beateworks: 35 tr; Tibor Bognar: 46 cl, 46 cl; Christophe Boisvieux: 17 br; Simonpietri Christian/ Corbis Sygma: 9 br; Arko Datta/Reuters: 46 cl; Colin Dixon/ Arcaid: 38 crb; DLILLC: 30 bc, 56 cr; epa: 14 cl; Alejandro Ernesto/epa: 14 bl; Randy Faris: 24 bl; Paddy Fields - Louie Psihoyos: 50 bl; Franz Marc Frei: 56 bl; Natalie Fobes: 35 br; Owen Franken: 17 tr; Darrell Gulin: 15 cr; Ainal Abd Halim/Reuters: 42 tr; Lindsay Hebberd: 17 tl; Chris Hellier: 31 cr; Dallas and John Heaton/ Free Agents Limited: 29 br, 49 tr; Jon Hicks: 27 br; Robert van der Hilst: 38 cl; Eric and David Hosking: 15 bcl; Hanan Isachar: 43 tr; Wolfgang Kaehler: 15 tl,15 br, 54 bl; Catherine Karnow: 38 cr, 55 tr; Frank Krahmer/ zefa: 27 cl; Jacques Langevin/Corbis Sygma: 41 tr; Danny Lehman: 25 br; John and Lisa Merrill: 36 c; Viviane Moos: 46 tr; Kazuyoshi Nomachi: 29 tc; Neil Rabinowitz: 57 cr; Finbarr O'Reilly/ Reuters: 16 tr; José Fuste Raga/zefa: 14 br, 22 bl, 34 cr, 49 br, 50 c; Carmen Redondo: 32 br; Reuters: 26 cr, 53 tr; Guenter Rossenbach/zefa: 15 tcl; Galen Rowell: 55 tl, 58 cr; Anders Ryman: 52 cl; Kevin Schafer: 9 bc; Alfio Scigliano/ Sygma/Corbis: 37 br; Paul Seheult/ Eye Ubiquitous: 26 tr, Hugh Sitton/ zefa: 51 tl; Hubert Stadler: 15 tcr; Paul A. Souders: 33 cr; Jon Sparks: 42 bl; Shannon Stapleton/Reuters: 16 bl; Hans Strand: 56 tr; Staffan Widstrand: 37 cr; Uli Wiesmeier/zefa: 36 tr; Tony Wharton/ Frank Lane Picture Agency: 37 tr; Larry Williams: 25 tr; Valdrin Xhemaj/epa: 21 tc; Shamil Zhumatov/Reuters: 44 c.

ESA: 8 cl, c, cr, 9 cl, c, ca, cr.

FLPA: Ingo Arndt/Foto NaturaI/Minden Pictures: 38 bc; Richard Becker: 14 tr; Jim Brandenburg/Minden Pictures: 48 cl; Hans Dieter Brandl: 32 cr; Michael Callan: 32 cl; R.Dirscherl: 51 cr; Gerry Ellis/Minden Pictures: 48 bl; im Fitzharris/Minden Pictures/FLPA: 20 bl; Michael & Patricia Fogden/Minden Pictures: 24 bc; Michael Gore: 52 c; Rev. Bruce Henry: 46 br; Michio Hoshino/Minden Pictures: 23 tr, 58 br; Mitsuaki Iwago /Minden Pictures: 52 bc; Frank W Lane: 45 tr; Frans Lanting: 23 bc, 26 bc, 29 cr; Thomas Mangelsen/ Minden Picture: 4-5 b; S & D & K Maslowski: 20 bc; Claus Meyer/Minden Pictures: 26 cl; Yva Momatiuk /John Eastcott/Minden Pictures: 27 tr; Colin Monteath /Minden Pictures: 47 tr; Rinie van Muers/Foto Natura: 3 c, 59 tr; Mark Newman: 41 tl; Flip Nicklin/Minden Picture: 21 tr; R & M Van Nostrand: 28 bl; Alan Parker: 44 bl; Walter Rohdich: 46 cr; L Lee Rue: 21 cr; Cyril Ruoso\JH Editorial/Minden Pictures: 36 br; Silvestris Fotoservice: 39 cr; Jurgen & Christine Sohns: 31 tc, 44 br; Inga Spence: 42 bc; Egmont Strigl/ Imagebroker/FLPA: 45 br; Chris & Tilde Stuart: 43 br; Terry Andrewartha: 58 tr; Barbara Todd/ Hedgehog House/ Minden Pictures: 59 cr; Winfried Wisniewski: 40 cl, 59 bl; Terry Whittaker: 34 tr; Konrad Wothe/Minden Pictures: 40 bc; Zhinong Xi/Minden Pictures: 49 tl; Shin Yoshino/Minden Pictures: 53 cr.

Andy Crawford: 51 br

Steve Gorton: 24 c, 34 cl, 36 c, 38 tc, bc, 41 bl, 42 c, 45 tl, cr, 47 cl, bc, 49 cr, 51 c, 54 tr, 54 tr, 54 bc

NASA: 9 tr, 23 br.
Chez Picthall: 2 b, 23 tc, 41 br.

Peter Picthall: 28 cl

Still Pictures: K. Thomas/Still Pictures: 39 tl

Warren Photographic: Jane Burton: 39 br, 50 tr, 57 br; Kim Taylor and Mark Taylor: 32 c; Mark Taylor: 50 tl, Monarch butterflies © Warren Photographic: 24 tc.

Dominic Zwemmer: 14 cl, 15 bc, 30 cl, 53 br, 57 ac

Front cover
Main image: NASA; Keith Binns/ iStockphoto: tl; Michael Gore FLPA: cl; Dominic Zwemmer: clb; Cyril Ruoso\ JHEditoria/Minden Pictures/FLPA: bl

Back cover
WarrenPhotographic: tl; NASA: bl.

All other images © of Picthall and Gunzi.

Every effort has been made to trace the copyright holders and we apologize in advance for any unintentional omissions. We would be pleased to insert the appropriate acknowledgement in any subsequent edition of this book.

Continents of the World

ATLANTIC
OCEAN

EUROPE

A S I A

ATLANTIC
OCEAN

AFRICA

INDIAN
OCEAN

AUSTR

S O U T H E R N   O C E A N

ANTARCTICA